Start Investing in Mutual Funds

Start Investing in Mutual Funds

Learn how to grow your money through simple, low-maintenance fund investing

Julian Renner

Mindful Pages

Published in 2025

ISBN: 9789371774727 (PB)
ISBN: 9789371772747 (eBook)

Published by

Mindful Pages
Imprint of Alpha Editions LLC
312 W. 2nd St #1834
Casper, WY 82601, USA

This book was developed using advanced writing tools to support the drafting and ideation process. All content has been thoughtfully curated, refined, and reviewed to ensure quality and relevance.

Content

Introduction Slow Money, Strong Roots viii

Chapter 1 The Case for Simple Wealth 1

Chapter 2 What Mutual Funds Really Are 23

Chapter 3 Meet the Fund Family 44

Chapter 4 The Wisdom of the Index 63

Chapter 5 Actively Managed Funds—When, Why, and If 81

Chapter 6 SIPs and the Psychology of Progress 98

Chapter 7 Risk Isn't What You Think It Is 115

Chapter 8 Choosing Your Fund, Choosing Your Future 133

Chapter 9 How to Actually Start Investing 151

Chapter 10 The Art of Doing Less, Better 167

Conclusion 184

About the Author 190

Introduction
Slow Money, Strong Roots

We live in an era where speed masquerades as progress. Algorithms execute trades in microseconds. Financial influencers flaunt daily wins across social media feeds. Brokerage apps buzz insistently, nudging you to act, react, optimise—constantly. Investing, once a patient craft aligned with the rhythms of life and growth, now often resembles a frantic scramble, a contest of prediction and performance. The prevailing narrative whispers that if you are not fast, you are behind; if not clever, you are exposed; if not constantly adjusting, you are losing out.

This book takes a different view.

Start Investing in Mutual Funds begins with a quietly countercultural assertion: lasting wealth—wealth that sustains lives, funds ambitions, and endures cycles—is rarely born from brilliance, bravado, or bold, headline-grabbing bets. It is cultivated through stillness, through repetition, through restraint. Through the kind of disciplined, emotionally grounded action that often escapes notice yet quietly compounds over time.

This is not a manual for beating the market. It is a guide to outgrowing the mindset that believes you must. The truth is at once humbling and liberating: you do not need to be a financial prodigy to secure your future. You need a clear, manageable strategy, the emotional fortitude to follow it, and, above all, time—both as a measured span and as a cultivated mindset. Time is your greatest financial ally, not a metric to be rushed.

The Hidden Cost of Complexity

Browse a bookstore or scroll through financial content online, and a message emerges loud and clear: investing is hard, intimidating, exclusionary. It is couched in acronyms, charts, volatility graphs, performance tables, and jargon, leaving the uninitiated feeling underqualified before they even begin. This complexity does not serve investors; it serves the industry.

When investing appears arcane, hesitation follows. People delay. They second-guess themselves. Fear of missteps paralyses action. And the cost is steep—not just financially, but emotionally. Anxiety creeps in as quiet stress. Guilt manifests for "wasted" earning years. Avoidance calcifies into inertia: "I'll start next year," "I'll learn enough first."

This book aims to break that cycle.

By demystifying mutual funds—one of the most accessible, low-barrier vehicles for everyday investors—it invites you to step confidently back into the conversation. Not as a passive observer, nor performing sophistication, but as someone choosing a calm, clear path forward.

Reframing Wealth: From Spectacle to Substance

Let us be candid: the cultural image of investing is distorted. It is too often portrayed as a test of cunning, ego, or aggression. From high-frequency traders to celebrity stock picks, attention gravitates to drama and temporary wins. These stories perpetuate the myth of the "market genius," suggesting that extraordinary insight, timing, or luck is required.

Yet these tales are exceptions, not templates.

Research consistently demonstrates that ordinary investors who commit to simple, long-term fund investing often outperform those chasing returns, timing the market, or constantly rebalancing. Not because they know more, but because they do less. They safeguard attention, anchor emotions, and create a system they can live with.

Here, investing is practice, not performance. It is not adrenaline-driven but aligned with your goals, values, and temperament. It is not a hunt for the perfect product or moment. It is disciplined consistency. It is the courage to reject noise and embrace stillness.

Why Mutual Funds—Why Now?

In a landscape crowded with options—cryptocurrencies, trading platforms, complex derivatives, robo-advisors—why focus on mutual funds? Because they work.

Properly chosen, mutual funds offer low-friction access to diversified, professionally managed portfolios. They relieve the individual of the burden of selection, spread risk, and allow customization across time horizons and risk appetites. They accommodate modest beginnings and compound quietly over decades. Most importantly, they align mathematical logic with emotional sustainability. They do not reward compulsion. They are a container for long-term wealth, structured, guided, and adaptable to real lives.

Yet not all funds are equal. Some are designed to serve investors; others to extract from them. This book seeks not only to explain mutual funds but to arm you with the discernment to identify those worthy of your trust.

Emotional Literacy as Financial Literacy

Beyond mechanics, investing is psychological. Anxiety, often not about money per se but about control, identity, and self-worth, underpins many poor financial decisions. Financial literacy alone cannot address this. Emotional literacy must accompany it.

Throughout these chapters, you will learn not only about fund types, market mechanics, and investment strategies, but also how to manage your emotional response to money. You will discover how to make peace with volatility, how to build portfolios compatible with your life and risk appetite, and how to embed calm and deliberation into your investing routine. Automation becomes not just a convenience, but a ritual of care. The hardest part—doing nothing at times—is often the most transformative.

Financial knowledge without emotional awareness is incomplete. You are not a machine executing models; you are a human navigating complexity. This book honours that reality.

What You Will—and Won't—Find Here

You will not encounter sensational predictions or breathless commentary. You will not be urged to chase returns or follow influencers.

Instead, you will find rigour, relevance, and realism. Mutual funds will be explained in plain language. You will learn to evaluate products, choose platforms, set goals, and track progress without obsession. You will see how simplicity in finances fosters emotional spaciousness, which allows wealth to grow quietly, steadily, reliably.

Each chapter removes barriers—mental, emotional, practical—that may have kept you from starting. You will confront invisible obstacles, learn how mutual funds function, understand different fund types and their psychological fit, dispel market myths, appreciate indexing, determine when active management makes sense, and design a systematic investment plan with intention. You will redefine risk to empower rather than frighten, building a portfolio you can inhabit and live by.

An Invitation to Begin, Slowly

This book is not here to dazzle; it is here to steady. It does not promise quick wins, but durable wisdom. It does not demand intensity, but rewards patience. It does not ask you to become someone else, but to align with what you already value: clarity, peace, security, and agency.

Think of this as an investment not merely in mutual funds, but in a new identity—as someone who no longer defers the future out of fear or fatigue. Someone willing to start slowly, plant steadily, and grow with intention.

Because real wealth is not chased. It is cultivated.

Welcome. Let us begin.

Chapter 1
The Case for Simple Wealth

Amid the relentless clatter of personal finance—apps pinging, headlines flashing, influencers proclaiming wins—a quiet truth persists: most people still do not invest. They may talk about it, open an account, or even intend to begin. Yet the steady act of setting aside money, choosing a fund, and maintaining course remains elusive. This is rarely about laziness or irresponsibility. The modern investment landscape, despite its apparent accessibility, can feel psychologically and systemically hostile. Fear, confusion, perfectionism, and ingrained beliefs about money conspire to keep capable, intelligent people on the sidelines.

To grasp the appeal of simple wealth, we must first confront the emotional architecture of hesitation. Fear is not merely about losing capital—it is the fear of looking foolish. Jargon is not just technical—it is alienating. The compulsion to get everything "exactly right" often overrides the more critical goal of simply starting. These anxieties are rational, given a financial culture designed more for spectacle than inclusion.

Mutual funds, properly understood, offer a remedy. They reduce the burden of constant decision-making. They replace drama with structure. They bridge the abstract world of investing with the tangible realities of everyday life. Yet to cross that bridge, we must acknowledge the terrain: the internal and external obstacles that have shaped our reluctance in the first place.

Much of what prevents people from beginning is not access or intellect—it is the emotional cost. Financial institutions and media often frame literacy in terms of charts, ratios, and returns. But human decision-making rarely begins with numbers; it begins with narrative. The prevailing story is that investing is risky, complicated, and best left to the "experts."

This narrative is neither neutral nor accidental. It reflects upbringing, media exposure, and subtle cues that suggest investing is the domain of high-stakes players. If you grew up around silent, fraught conversations about money, investing can feel intrusive. If you have long associated wealth with greed or detachment, you may unconsciously resist it even while seeking stability. Add the dizzying array of funds, platforms, and opinions, and it is no surprise that many defer action. What appears as procrastination is often simply emotional overload.

This chapter seeks to clear that fog—not through checklists, but by reframing wealth creation itself. Investing need not be complex, intimidating, or heroic. Enduring success arises not from rare insight or insider access, but from sustained simplicity. The stories here are of quiet compounding, of everyday people learning to trust process over prediction.

The myth of the "market genius" persists because it appeals to a primal desire: to feel exceptional. To believe that with sufficient cleverness, one can outsmart the system. Yet the data is sobering. The majority of professional fund managers—highly trained, well-resourced, analytical—fail to consistently outperform the market over decades. If they cannot reliably do so, what does that imply for the rest of us?

The answer is liberation, not despair. Exceptional talent is not the gatekeeper of wealth. The difference lies in time—how it is treated, how it is respected. Compounding is behavioural as much as mathematical. It rewards calm over cleverness, consistency over creativity. In this sense, investing is less about what you know and more about what you repeat.

Repetition, however, is dull—and dull does not sell. Financial media thrives on novelty: new funds, hot sectors, imminent corrections. These narratives seize attention but breed insecurity, implying the need for constant action. Yet doing nothing—staying invested month after month, year after year—should not be mistaken for passivity. In investing, boredom is discipline.

Mutual funds, particularly index and broad-market options, enable this "strategic boredom." They allow investors to outsource complexity while focusing on what matters: contribution, consistency, and emotional resilience. They are imperfect, yes, but structurally aligned with long-term behaviour and accessible enough to remove the most persistent excuse: that you are not ready.

Readiness, in wealth-building, is largely an illusion. The market does not wait for confidence or perfection. Those who succeed are not the most prepared—they are those who begin with imperfection and refine over time. Preparation often masquerades as avoidance; starting is the true act of agency.

The shift from anxiety to agency begins with small acts of self-trust: establishing an SIP, reading a fund fact sheet, asking "How can I stay invested when uncertain?" rather than "How can I get rich?" These are subtle but decisive steps, signalling a move from passive worry to active alignment.

Consider a young professional contributing £100 per month to a broad equity fund from age 25. Over forty years, assuming an 8% annual return, this grows to over £300,000. Now imagine someone starting at 35, contributing £200 per month for thirty years: they reach just over £280,000. The earlier, smaller contributions outperform. Time, not size or sophistication, is the engine.

The lesson is profound: you need not be first or brilliant—just early and steady. In a culture fixated on performance, this is radical. Yet it is empowering. Time, unlike talent, is a resource anyone can harness.

This chapter also challenges the notion that investing equates to control—over outcomes, timing, or markets. True control arises from protection: of time, attention, and habits. Mutual funds offer precisely this. They shield you from reactive impulses and allow decisions to be automated, giving life back its freedom from constant net-worth scrutiny.

Financial calm is not risk-free; it is alignment. When strategy fits your goals, lifestyle, and emotional bandwidth, the compulsion to monitor every market twitch disappears. You have already decided what matters and established a system to uphold that choice.

The invitation here is to redefine wealth: not as outperforming others, but as consistency with yourself. To begin where you are, not where you imagine you should be. To reject the myth of lone genius in favour of the quiet strength of discipline. To embrace tools—mutual funds—that reflect both humility and wisdom.

Simple wealth is not lesser wealth. It is often the only kind most people truly build. It is not avoidance of effort, but the application of effort in the right place, once, and then letting it compound. It is about recognising risk, outsourcing what can be delegated, and choosing clarity over complexity.

This chapter is the first step toward that clarity. Not by teaching mastery over markets, but by helping you stop chasing it. By its conclusion, the case for simple wealth may seem less a tactic than a philosophy: an orientation of financial life around sustainable principles. And within that sustainability lies something more valuable than returns alone: peace.

Why Most People Never Start

The idea of investing evokes a peculiar kind of hesitation—one that persists even among highly educated, capable individuals. Ask a group of professionals about their views on investing and you're likely to hear a blend of guilt, confusion, and vague aspiration. Most know they *should* be doing it. Many have read articles, downloaded apps, or even opened investment accounts. Yet for a vast number, the act of actually investing—of selecting a fund, committing a regular amount, and staying with it—never quite materialises. Not because they are indifferent, but because something deeper is at play.

At first glance, this hesitation seems irrational. After all, compound growth is mathematically persuasive. The earlier one starts, the more time does the heavy lifting. Platforms have become cheaper, digital access easier. But this surface-level logic fails to acknowledge the emotional and psychological weight that investing carries for many people. What appears to be procrastination is more accurately a by-product of fear, perfectionism, systemic opacity, and inherited financial narratives—forces powerful enough to override even the most well-intentioned efforts.

We cannot solve this inertia through education alone. Nor can we dismiss it as laziness or ignorance. The barriers that prevent most people from investing are not simply informational—they are *emotional*, *cultural*, and *behavioural*. To address them, we must understand them in full.

The Fear Beneath the Numbers

Fear is perhaps the most underestimated force in the investment equation. It often manifests subtly: as overthinking, as endless research, as an inability to make a decision. But its roots run deep. At its core, the fear is not just about losing money—it is about *getting it wrong*. About feeling naive. About exposing oneself to an arena perceived to be dominated by experts, insiders, and people who understand codes you were never taught.

For many, money itself is emotionally charged. It is tied to childhood memories, to family dynamics, to self-worth. When people say they are "bad with money," they're rarely referring to arithmetic. They're describing a long-standing narrative of inadequacy. Investing, then, is not merely a financial decision—it is a confrontation with that narrative.

Consider the experience of a first-generation investor—someone whose parents never invested, perhaps never even had a formal bank account. For them, investing may feel not only unfamiliar but presumptuous. It carries the psychological weight of crossing into an unfamiliar world, one that wasn't built with their history or values in mind. Even the language of investing—terms like "asset allocation," "expense ratio," "diversification"—can feel like a foreign tongue. And like any new language, fluency requires exposure, patience, and an environment that doesn't punish early mistakes.

The Paralysis of Perfectionism

Ironically, it is often the most conscientious and well-informed individuals who fall prey to perfectionism. The desire to make the *best* investment decision—rather than a *good enough* one—frequently leads to inaction. These are the people who read market reports, compare fund performance, and yet, never press "invest." Their questions are endless: Is now the right time? Should I wait for the next market dip? What if I pick the wrong fund? What if I miss a better opportunity tomorrow?

This hyper-analysis, often mistaken for diligence, is in fact a disguised form of fear. Perfectionism is not about high standards—it is about avoidance. It creates a loop of endless preparation, where action is always one step away. And the cost is enormous. Because when it comes to compounding, the single greatest asset is time—not precision.

Mutual funds, particularly diversified equity and index funds, offer an elegant solution to this dilemma. They do not require you to be right about timing or market sectors. They do not demand predictive genius. What they ask for instead is regularity, patience, and the ability to trust in structure over speculation. In short, they reward humility. And humility, unlike perfectionism, permits action.

The Weaponisation of Jargon

Financial services, for all their modern user interfaces, remain steeped in complexity. This complexity is not always necessary—but it is often profitable for those who benefit from opacity. Investors are sold products they do not understand, under terms they cannot compare, and within structures that make exit inconvenient or costly. The average fund fact sheet, though legally required to disclose key information, is rarely designed to foster comprehension. Instead, it reassures through formality while deterring true scrutiny.

The result is a financial culture that is, at best, alienating—and at worst, exclusionary. Jargon becomes a gatekeeper, reinforcing the idea that investing is the domain of specialists. Terms like "alpha," "Sharpe ratio," and "quantitative easing" are not inherently problematic—but the context in which they are introduced often signals superiority, not education.

Mutual funds, especially when explained without theatricality, have the power to dismantle this barrier. They reframe investing as a group activity, not a solo performance. Instead of picking stocks or betting on outcomes, mutual fund investors participate in pooled, professionally managed vehicles where risk is shared, and strategy is systematic. The barrier to entry is not technical skill, but the willingness to trust a slow, repeatable process.

The Inheritance of Belief

Every investor brings to the table not only their income and risk tolerance, but also their financial conditioning—what they learned, directly or indirectly, about money growing up. Some inherited caution, having watched parents weather economic instability. Others inherited disdain, associating wealth with selfishness or corruption. Still others inherited silence, where money was simply never discussed.

These inherited beliefs shape financial behaviour more than we admit. They dictate how much risk feels appropriate, how much control feels necessary, and whether wealth itself feels like a welcome outcome or a betrayal of one's upbringing. An individual raised in a household where money was scarce may find it difficult to part with any disposable income—even if it's being invested for the future. Conversely, someone who grew up around financial abundance may treat investing as a casual hobby rather than a serious commitment.

What mutual funds offer in this context is not just access, but *emotional permission.* They allow individuals to invest without posturing, without pretending to have all the answers. They shift the focus from performance to participation—from beating the market to building a future. In doing so, they help to rewrite old scripts and create new associations. Investing no longer has to mean gambling. It can mean discipline. It can mean care.

From the Outside In

There is also a structural angle to all of this—barriers that are not psychological but institutional. In many countries, the financial system is skewed in favour of those who already have access: to education, to advisers, to early capital. Wealth begets wealth, not just through returns, but through knowledge, networks, and the capacity to take calculated risks without existential consequences.

For the everyday saver or first-time investor, this system can feel impenetrable. Banks push savings accounts, not equity funds. Media outlets spotlight success stories, rarely the years of quiet accumulation behind them. And most financial advisers are incentivised not by your best interest, but by commissions on specific products.

Mutual funds are not immune to this distortion—there are plenty of high-fee, underperforming funds marketed aggressively to the unsuspecting. But at their core, the mutual fund structure is fundamentally democratic. It was designed to allow many people to participate in markets that were once reserved for a privileged few. When low-cost, transparent, and properly chosen, mutual funds lower the bar to entry in both literal and symbolic ways. They offer not only affordability, but *accessibility*—the kind that says, "This is for you too."

The Cost of Delay

If the risks of investing are often overestimated, the risks of not investing are almost always underestimated. Inflation erodes the purchasing power of savings. Opportunity costs compound silently.

A decade without investment is not just a decade lost—it is a multiplier effect gone unrealised. And yet, because the consequences of inaction are invisible in the short term, they rarely motivate behaviour change.

This is why emotional friction matters so much. The longer someone hesitates, the more difficult it becomes to begin. Delays calcify into avoidance. Avoidance becomes identity: "*I'm just not an investing person.*" And the longer this narrative is reinforced, the harder it becomes to dismantle.

The antidote is not pressure—it is orientation. A small SIP, a modest index fund, a simplified account setup—these are not insignificant steps. They are the beginning of a new pattern, one rooted not in reaction, but in intention. They represent a redefinition of what it means to participate in wealth creation—not as a performance, but as a quiet, self-respecting act.

A Way Through, Not Around

To move from hesitation to action, people don't need to become experts. They need to *feel safe enough to begin.* Mutual funds, particularly when approached with clarity and care, provide that safety net. They lower the emotional cost of investing by reducing decision fatigue, insulating against volatility, and offering built-in diversification. More importantly, they allow for the development of a repeatable habit—one that prioritises consistency over brilliance.

This subchapter is not a defence of simplicity for its own sake. It is a defence of simplicity as a response to complexity that no longer serves. When we strip away the jargon, dismantle perfectionism, and reject inherited financial shame, what remains is a remarkably straightforward question: *How can I participate in building my own future—without needing to control every variable?*

Mutual funds offer a practical, principled answer. And for many, they are not just a product—they are a permission slip to start.

The Myth of the Market Genius

The public imagination has long been seduced by the figure of the market genius: a sharp-suited individual who sees patterns where others see noise, who times trades to perfection, and who, through sheer intellect or instinct, outsmarts the financial system. This archetype—half analyst, half mystic—has become the dominant cultural story about how wealth is built through investing. It is not only a fiction. It is a dangerous one. Because while it flatters our desire to feel special, it misrepresents how most lasting fortunes are actually created. The market is not a stage for brilliance. It is a testing ground for behaviour. And when it comes to real-world investing outcomes, *humility outperforms bravado every time.*

The belief in genius investors is not limited to late-night stock tip shows or speculative YouTube channels. It permeates respected institutions. Media headlines spotlight hedge fund titans, contrarian bets, and singular trades that yielded exponential gains. Business books elevate individuals who "predicted" market crashes or identified obscure opportunities before they went mainstream. The implicit lesson is clear: to succeed, you must *see what others don't.* You must be exceptional.

But investing is not a creativity contest. It is a discipline of repetition, risk control, and emotional steadiness. The data are unequivocal: the vast majority of actively managed funds underperform the market over time. In the most extensive studies—such as the SPIVA (S&P Indices Versus Active) scorecards published annually—roughly 80 to 90 percent of actively managed equity funds fail to beat their benchmarks over ten- and fifteen-year periods. In some asset classes and geographies, the failure rate is even higher. This is not a temporary phenomenon. It is structural. The odds are not only unfavourable—they are mathematically rigged against consistent outperformance.

What often gets overlooked is that investing involves more friction than theory suggests. There are fees, taxes, liquidity constraints, behavioural pitfalls, and timing errors. The moment we shift from spreadsheets to human behaviour, a new picture emerges. It's not about who knows the most—it's about who *interferes the least.* The winning strategy, repeated across case studies and time periods, is not intellectual superiority but behavioural consistency.

Take the example of index funds. Introduced by John Bogle in the 1970s, they were initially dismissed as anti-intellectual—an option for those who had neither the skill nor the interest to "beat" the market. And yet, over the decades, index funds have quietly and overwhelmingly outperformed the vast majority of actively managed funds. Not by anticipating market moves, but by *not trying to.* Their success is rooted not in insight, but in structure. By tracking broad indices, maintaining low fees, and eliminating manager error, they remove the very variables that cause most investors to underperform.

The irony is rich: the so-called "lazy" approach turns out to be the most effective. Not because it is clever, but because it is *unpretentious.* It acknowledges what behavioural economists have long demonstrated—that humans are terrible at predicting markets and even worse at knowing when to get in or out. The more decisions you make, the more likely you are to make the wrong ones. Resisting this impulse requires not more knowledge, but *less self-regard.*

There is an instructive parallel here with medicine. The most effective medical protocols—checklists in surgery, standardised antibiotic prescriptions—are often criticised for being unglamorous. But they work because they *systematically reduce the room for error.* In the same way, a well-structured, low-maintenance investment plan outperforms sporadic brilliance because it removes the need for constant interpretation. The best investors are often the ones who design systems that remove themselves from the equation.

It is tempting, of course, to believe we are the exception. To think that our background in finance, or our intuition, or our network gives us an edge. But markets are relentlessly efficient in ways that undermine even the most well-informed actors. The moment information becomes known, it is priced in. The moment an edge becomes visible, it is competed away. And for retail investors especially, the asymmetry of information and execution means that whatever advantage one imagines having is usually illusory.

This isn't to say that no one can beat the market. Some do, for a while. A very small subset of investors—such as Renaissance Technologies or Warren Buffett's Berkshire Hathaway—have generated long-term alpha. But these are *statistical anomalies*, not templates for action. Their outperformance is the product of specific circumstances, structural advantages, and often, a willingness to accept immense volatility that most individuals could not stomach. Even Buffett himself has famously encouraged average investors to stick to low-cost index funds—recognising that the tools that built his fortune are neither replicable nor appropriate for most.

More instructive than chasing genius is studying those who became wealthy through disciplined, unflashy accumulation. Consider Grace Groner, a secretary who invested modestly in blue-chip stocks, reinvested dividends, and avoided selling for decades. When she passed away, she left millions to a charitable foundation. Her story made headlines precisely because it was so dissonant: how could someone with no financial training outperform so many so-called professionals? The answer, as always, lies not in timing or selection—but in *patience and consistency*.

Humility in investing is not weakness. It is an *epistemological position*—a recognition of what we cannot know, and an embrace of strategies that work in spite of that ignorance. It is the willingness to say: I don't know what the market will do tomorrow, but I do know how to build a portfolio that will serve me over decades. That's not defeatism. That's wisdom.

There is also an ethical dimension to rejecting the cult of the genius investor. It reframes success as a process, not a persona. It shifts the focus from spectacle to sustainability. In a world where financial discourse is increasingly performative—where success is displayed on screens and portfolios are paraded like trophies—the idea of quiet compounding is profoundly subversive. It says: you don't need to outsmart anyone. You just need to *outlast* them.

This matters because when we deconstruct the myth of the market genius, we democratise investing. We make space for the cautious, the busy, the non-expert. We allow people to participate without performance anxiety. Mutual funds, especially low-cost index and diversified equity funds, are the instruments that make this possible. They allow for regular, automated contributions. They minimise the need for ongoing analysis. And they reward long-term engagement over short-term excitement.

The cultural shift this invites is significant. It means redefining what it means to be a "smart" investor. Not the one with the most exotic picks, but the one with the most robust system. Not the one who boasts about returns, but the one who *shows up every month, without fail.* Intelligence in investing is not about knowing more—it's about acting better. And acting better, more often than not, means doing less.

There is a final illusion that sustains the genius myth: the belief that financial success must be difficult, esoteric, or exclusive. That to be valuable, a strategy must also be complex. But this reflects a broader societal bias, one that confuses complication with sophistication. The best ideas in any field—whether science, engineering, or finance—are often elegantly simple. They persist not because they dazzle, but because they endure.

The same holds true in investing. Mutual funds, when understood properly, are the financial equivalent of clean drinking water: unremarkable in their presentation, but revolutionary in their impact. They allow anyone, regardless of background or bandwidth, to [illegible]te meaningfully in wealth creation. They ask for no genius—[illegible]ision, and the discipline to repeat it.

The myth of the market genius may continue to sell books, attract followers, and populate headlines. But its shelf life is limited. Eventually, reality reasserts itself. Portfolios either grow through compounding, or they shrink through overreach. The difference is rarely knowledge. It is almost always *behaviour.* And behaviour, unlike brilliance, can be learned, trained, and embedded.

If there is a skill worth cultivating in investing, it is not cleverness. It is restraint. Not prediction, but process. Not aggression, but alignment. These are the traits that produce durable outcomes—not because they sound impressive, but because they work. Consistently. Quietly. And across lifetimes.

Wealth as a Function of Time, Not Talent

If you handed two people the same amount of money to invest, but gave one of them a decade's head start, the final difference in their portfolios would likely dwarf anything talent could account for. Time, not intelligence, is the dominant variable in wealth creation. It's an uncomfortable truth in a culture obsessed with optimisation and intellectual superiority—but it's a liberating one. Because while talent is rare and hard to define, time is democratic. It is available in unequal portions, yes, but its mechanism—compounding—is available to anyone willing to start early and persist long enough.

The investment world tends to celebrate decision-makers, analysts, and predictors—the ones who spot trends and move fast. But if you examine the actual outcomes of wealth building over decades, a different story emerges. Those who begin early, contribute consistently, and resist the urge to over-manage almost always outperform more reactive, tactically talented investors who start later or trade frequently. The defining skill is not selection—it's *duration.*

Consider two hypothetical investors: Investor A starts at age 25, investing £200 a month in a low-cost equity mutual fund. Investor B, more financially literate and with a higher income, waits until age 35 but invests £400 a month—double the amount. Assuming an average annual return of 8%, by age 65, Investor A will have contributed £96,000 and end up with approximately £622,000. Investor B will have contributed the same amount—£144,000 over 30 years—but will end up with about £489,000. The earlier, smaller investor wins, not through strategy or skill, but through *patience and proximity to compounding.*

This is not theoretical. It is mathematically repeatable. The early years of compounding are deceptively unimpressive; the later years are disproportionately powerful. Yet most people delay investing until they feel "ready"—as though understanding everything is a prerequisite for participating. It isn't. What matters most is giving your money time to grow in a system that rewards stillness over cleverness.

The power of compounding is intuitive when applied to debt—interest on credit cards or loans feels oppressive precisely because it multiplies quietly and relentlessly. But when applied to assets, it requires a shift in psychological framing. It demands faith in slow accumulation over spectacle. It challenges the belief that knowledge must be translated into constant action. This is why many highly intelligent people underperform as investors. They assume that complexity must yield better results. It doesn't.

One of the most cited studies on investor performance comes from research conducted by DALBAR, a financial analytics firm. Their long-term analysis consistently shows that the average investor earns significantly less than the market—not because of the products they choose, but because of the behaviours they exhibit. Buying high after media hype, selling low after downturns, switching funds out of impatience or panic—these actions stem not from ignorance, but from *overconfidence in one's ability to time decisions.* Talent, in these cases, is not just ineffective. It's counterproductive.

By contrast, mutual funds—particularly broad-market index or equity funds—function as a discipline device. They offer a structure through which time can operate unimpeded. The investor does not need to predict anything. They simply need to *participate and persist.* A systematic investment plan (SIP) tied to monthly contributions becomes not a tactical move, but a behavioural contract. It aligns with cash flow, reduces timing risk, and turns wealth-building into a lifestyle rather than a performance.

This reframing is crucial. If investing is about talent, it becomes exclusive. It's something you're either good at or not. But if investing is about time, then it becomes inclusive. The right question is no longer, *What should I know before starting?* but *How soon can I afford to begin?* It levels the field—not by erasing skill, but by recognising that skill is secondary to behaviour in long-term investing outcomes.

We see this clearly in the biographies of real investors. Warren Buffett—arguably the most iconic name in modern investing—is not revered primarily because of his stock picks. His genius lies in the fact that he started investing as a child and remained invested for over seven decades. More than 90 percent of his net worth was accumulated after his 65th birthday. His annualised returns are exceptional, yes—but the real magic is the *time* those returns had to operate.

Similarly, everyday investors who achieve financial independence rarely do so through sudden windfalls or tactical brilliance. They do so through automated investing, regular contributions, and minimal interference. Consider the case of Sylvia Bloom, a legal secretary who amassed over $9 million by living modestly and investing in the same funds she watched the firm's lawyers buy. Her wealth was built not by forecasting or frequent trades, but by allowing her money to grow uninterrupted over decades. Her story, while remarkable in scale, is not unique in structure.

The implications for strategy are clear. The most underutilised asset in wealth creation is *time in the market*, not timing the market. This distinction is often misunderstood. Timing implies anticipation; duration implies endurance. One requires predictive accuracy; the other requires emotional maturity. And maturity, unlike brilliance, can be cultivated with effort and intention.

This orientation also allows for better planning. When you understand that time amplifies small decisions, you gain confidence in modest beginnings. You do not need large sums to start investing. A small SIP started early and sustained with discipline can rival—and often exceed—the results of lump-sum investments started too late. It creates not only financial growth but psychological anchoring. You begin to see yourself as someone who invests, not because of expertise, but because of alignment with your future self.

This mindset is increasingly important in a world of financial distraction. Every day, new products, platforms, and strategies promise better returns. The temptation to switch, optimise, or chase performance is ever-present. But those who internalise the function of time as the key driver of wealth learn to mute that noise. They do not chase perfection. They commit to *sufficiency executed consistently*.

There is also a moral clarity in this approach. It counters the narrative that financial success is a function of rare insight or insider knowledge. It affirms that ordinary people, acting patiently, can achieve extraordinary results. Not through shortcuts, but through steady steps taken early and often. It reconnects wealth to values—discipline, patience, and respect for future needs—not speculation or supremacy.

The behavioural aspect cannot be overstated. Investing through mutual funds is not simply about market exposure; it is about habit formation. It builds a cadence into one's financial life—monthly contributions, periodic reviews, automatic reinvestments. This rhythm becomes protective. It removes the decision fatigue that derails so many would-be investors. It offers a counterpoint to the anxiety-inducing volatility of markets. When you trust time, you stop needing control. You stop needing constant feedback. You start playing a longer game.

If there is a single idea that should guide investment behaviour, it is this: *starting early beats being smart.* No spreadsheet model, no technical analysis, no market insight can replicate the effect of years added to the compounding timeline. And while we cannot turn back the clock, we can refuse to delay further. The best day to start was yesterday. The second-best is still today.

This is not a call for passivity. It is a call for *intelligent surrender*—to systems that work over time, to principles that scale, and to strategies that require fewer decisions, not more. Mutual funds offer that structure. Time does the rest.

Talent may impress, but it rarely endures. Time, on the other hand, is relentless, impartial, and always working. Those who align with it gain more than just returns—they gain freedom from the myth that investing must be complex or performative. They step out of the theatre and into the field—quiet, steady, and enduringly effective.

From Anxiety to Agency

For many, the subject of money is not merely practical—it is profoundly emotional. Financial decisions are rarely just arithmetic; they are laced with memory, identity, expectation, and fear. When we think about investing, the default emotional state is not confidence—it is unease. Even among well-informed professionals, the gap between knowing what to do and actually doing it is often filled with silent dread: fear of making a mistake, of losing what little has been saved, of appearing naive, or of exposing a fundamental inadequacy. Beneath this lies a more universal anxiety—the sense that money is always slightly out of control, no matter how hard we try to manage it.

This emotional state is not irrational. In fact, it is a reasonable reaction to a system that often feels opaque, volatile, and designed for those with more time, knowledge, or nerve. Investing, particularly for first-time or reluctant participants, can feel like being asked to play a game without knowing the rules—while being told that getting it wrong could be disastrous. The result is a state of low-grade, chronic financial anxiety: a hum in the background of adult life that rarely becomes a crisis, but never quite goes away.

The cultural signals around investing amplify this discomfort. Most financial discourse focuses on what to do—buy this, avoid that, watch out for the next crash. Less attention is paid to *how it feels* to engage with money over time, and even less to how emotional patterns shape long-term financial outcomes. The industry remains deeply technical in language and aspirational in tone, leaving ordinary investors feeling that they must either become experts or surrender control entirely. This creates a false binary: either you are "good with money," or you're destined to be passive, vulnerable, and dependent.

Mutual funds, especially when understood not as products but as frameworks, offer a third path—one that leads from anxiety to agency. They are not simply a way to access the market. They are a way to lower the emotional cost of investing by outsourcing complexity and automating discipline. The benefit is not only financial but psychological: a gradual but decisive shift from stress to strategy, from fear to functional control.

Agency, in this context, does not mean total control. It means *appropriate control.* It means choosing a system that works for you without requiring daily vigilance or constant optimisation. It means acknowledging the limits of your time, attention, and emotional bandwidth, and building a structure that supports, rather than undermines, your long-term objectives. Mutual funds, by design, allow this. They transform investing from a high-stakes decision into a sustainable habit.

Take the example of someone in their thirties who has avoided investing because the process feels overwhelming. They know, abstractly, that they "should be doing something." But every attempt to research the options ends in decision fatigue. The language is dense, the fees are buried, and the stakes feel too high to move forward without full confidence. They remain in a cycle of inaction—not because they lack willpower, but because the cost of engaging feels greater than the cost of waiting. This is the definition of financial paralysis.

Now consider what happens when that same person is introduced to a low-cost index mutual fund, paired with a monthly SIP (Systematic Investment Plan). Suddenly, the decision shrinks from a sprawling forest of variables into a clear, repeatable action. There is no need to pick stocks. No requirement to watch the news. No compulsion to time the market. The investor no longer needs to *know everything*. They simply need to decide *once*, set an amount, and let the system do what it's built to do.

This transition—this psychological demotion of self from constant manager to strategic architect—is where real agency begins. It is a form of control precisely because it relinquishes the illusion of control over every market movement. And this is a radical departure from what many assume investing requires. The shift is not from ignorance to mastery, but from obsession to order. That order brings calm.

To treat investing as a form of financial self-respect is to view it not as a gamble, or a game, but as a dignified act of care. It is not about outperforming peers or reaching some arbitrary number. It is about aligning your financial decisions with your values, goals, and limitations. When mutual funds are chosen for their fit—diversified, low-cost, appropriate to your risk tolerance—they become an anchor, not a burden. They help translate abstract hopes into concrete behaviours.

The deeper insight here is that financial calm is not the absence of risk—it is the presence of a framework that holds risk in proportion. The market will always fluctuate. But anxiety doesn't have to. When the strategy is built to weather volatility, you are no longer emotionally hijacked by every downturn. You can acknowledge the red on your portfolio without internalising it as a personal failure.

That separation—between what the market does and what it means about you—is one of the most powerful shifts an investor can make.

This is not merely a philosophical reframing. It has behavioural consequences. Investors who are less anxious make fewer impulsive decisions. They are more likely to stay invested through downturns. They are less susceptible to the fear-greed cycle that drives poor performance over time. In fact, the very act of creating a low-maintenance investment plan can reduce the cognitive load associated with money, freeing up mental and emotional energy for other parts of life. The benefits compound in more ways than just returns.

There is also a collective relevance to this emotional arc. For those raised in environments where money was scarce, unstable, or a source of conflict, the idea of investing can feel not only foreign but morally ambiguous. It can trigger guilt ("Shouldn't I be using this money now?"), fear ("What if I lose everything?"), or shame ("I don't know what I'm doing, and I should"). These reactions are not irrational. They are the remnants of economic trauma. To invest through mutual funds—safely, sustainably, and steadily—is to reframe wealth-building as a healing act. It is to say: *I deserve to have a future.* And not one dictated by stress or scarcity.

This reframing is particularly urgent in a financial system that often punishes the uninitiated. Hidden fees, aggressive marketing, and predatory products thrive on confusion and urgency. Mutual funds, at their best, are a rare counterweight to that. They are designed not for thrills, but for endurance. Their appeal is not emotional drama, but structural clarity. They do not eliminate risk, but they contextualise it—through diversification, professional management, and built-in discipline.

Letting go of control to build real control may sound paradoxical, but it reflects one of the core principles of mature investing. You do not need to control every variable. You need to control the few that matter: your savings rate, your time horizon, your fund choice, and your emotional reactivity. Mutual funds, when used wisely, reinforce this focus. They remove noise. They reduce the need for micro-management. They encourage a posture of enough.

This posture has profound implications. When your investments are set up to work independently of your mood, your schedule, or the headlines, you reclaim energy. You stop thinking of money as something to monitor constantly and start thinking of it as something to build around. You become less reactive, more deliberate. Less anxious, more aligned. This is not just a financial shift—it is an existential one.

The path from anxiety to agency is not a single leap. It is a process of re-education, reorientation, and redefinition. It asks us to update old scripts—about who investing is for, about what it demands, and about what it gives back. It invites us to stop performing competence and instead *build confidence*—quietly, gradually, and with tools designed to support rather than overwhelm.

In this context, mutual funds are not a compromise or a beginner's crutch. They are a manifestation of strategic maturity. They signal a refusal to gamble, a refusal to delay, and a refusal to outsource your financial future to chance or charisma. They represent a kind of dignity—the dignity of being prepared, being protected, and being focused on what matters.

To invest through mutual funds is to trust time over timing, structure over impulse, and sufficiency over spectacle. It is not a relinquishment of responsibility. It is a reclamation of control—measured, mindful, and resilient. From that foundation, anxiety recedes. Agency rises. And the future, however uncertain, becomes something you are not just hoping for—but *building towards*.

Chapter 2
What Mutual Funds Really Are

Mutual funds, despite their frequent mention in discussions about personal finance, remain widely misunderstood. Too often, they are dismissed as bland instruments—"safe," "diversified," convenient placeholders in an investor's toolkit—rarely appreciated for what they truly represent: a sophisticated, democratically structured avenue for wealth creation. This chapter aims to do more than explain mechanics; it seeks to illuminate mutual funds as vehicles of collective empowerment, emotional discipline, and broad accessibility.

At their essence, mutual funds pool the resources of many individual investors. Each participant contributes a portion of capital, which is then managed by professional fund managers who allocate it across a portfolio of equities, bonds, or a combination thereof, according to the fund's stated mandate. Investors hold proportional units, sharing both gains and losses. The structure works not because each participant is an expert, but because it channels complexity through professional stewardship and shared opportunity.

The model is deceptively simple, yet its impact is profound. Imagine a mutual fund as a guided hiking expedition. Alone, you might venture only along familiar paths, constrained by risk and experience. In a coordinated group, with expert leadership, safety protocols, and logistical support, your range expands. You proceed steadily, buffered against impulsive decisions. You may not be the fastest, but you are far more likely to reach your destination intact.

Mutual funds derive their power not from promise, but from prevention. They mitigate the most perilous tendencies of individual investors: overreaction, concentration, and the illusion of superior knowledge. Unlike stock-picking, where timing and selection fall entirely on the individual, mutual funds outsource these responsibilities to professionals, diversify risk across multiple securities, and follow disciplined mandates. Emotional highs and lows are tempered by structural safeguards.

Evidence supports this advantage. Research, including insights underpinning Eugene Fama's Nobel-winning work, shows that individual investors—prone to overconfidence, loss aversion, and herd behaviour—consistently underperform the funds in which they invest. This "behaviour gap" demonstrates that losses often arise not from faulty products, but from emotional decision-making and poor timing. Mutual funds, particularly when accessed through regular contributions like SIPs, provide a behavioural counterweight, enabling investors to remain committed through downturns and harness the quiet power of compounding.

Yet opacity remains a challenge. Many investors cannot explain what occurs once their money enters a fund. This is a failure of communication, not of the product itself. A well-constructed mutual fund is transparent, and understanding its mechanics is both possible and empowering. Capital is aggregated, allocated according to the fund's objective—be it large-cap equities, mid-cap growth stocks, government bonds, or a diversified blend—and managed by professionals. Active funds rely on research and discretion; passive funds track indices. Fund performance is measured through the Net Asset Value (NAV), updated daily, and distributions—dividends, interest, or capital gains—are returned or reinvested depending on the plan.

This architecture introduces a crucial mental shift. Owning mutual fund units differs from holding individual shares. You do not control individual assets; you hold a proportional claim on the fund. Risk and return are mediated through diversification and professional management. Your exposure is indirect yet structured, which is where safety resides.

Safety, however, is not immunity. Costs exist: the expense ratio, entry and exit loads, turnover costs, and distribution fees. Passive index funds may charge under 0.2%, while active funds often exceed 1.5%, which compounds over decades. Understanding these costs is not paranoia—it is necessary diligence. Not all funds are created with the investor's interest at heart. Scrutiny requires asking: Is the cost justified by performance? Does the mandate align with my goals and risk tolerance? Is marketing obscuring execution quality?

Philosophically, mutual funds exemplify collective financial intelligence. They allow ordinary professionals—nurses, teachers, engineers, freelancers—to participate in markets without becoming full-time analysts. Beyond convenience, they provide economic enfranchisement, reducing dependence on inherited knowledge or insider access. Yet this accessibility carries responsibility: investors must engage deliberately, favouring longevity over spectacle. Mutual funds offer control over process, not outcomes—a distinction that is central to financial mastery.

The shift from speculative to strategic thinking manifests in disciplined portfolios. Automated contributions, occasional rebalancing, and attention to long-term objectives consistently outperform reactive investors chasing trends. Mutual funds facilitate this approach, systematising good behaviour, removing the need to guess, and transforming fragile triumphs into enduring progress.

As this chapter unfolds, we will dissect mutual funds: the journey of a single pound, the decisions made on your behalf, and how value accrues to you. We will explore behavioural benefits, examine cost structures, and provide simple filters to distinguish meaningful funds from polished distractions. The goal is to clarify not only the mechanics of mutual funds but also their economic, behavioural, and philosophical significance.

Financial writing often resorts to metaphors that sentimentalise complex instruments, but this chapter resists that temptation. Mutual funds are neither magical nor foolproof. They are rational tools, grounded in decades of research, bridging the gap between ordinary investors and the potential of capital markets. Their strength lies in simplicity; their promise lies in structure.

Crucially, mutual funds reward consistency over brilliance. For investors who commit to steady action, minimal interference, and a long horizon, they provide a plan that endures—through volatility, headline frenzy, and the temptation to act unnecessarily. Their true power is not complexity, but the clarity they offer to those willing to engage with them deliberately.

The Collective Engine of Mutual Funds

One of the most overlooked truths in investing is that most people, most of the time, are better served by joining forces than going it alone. Despite the enduring myth of the lone stock-picker triumphing against the odds, the vast majority of enduring wealth is not built through solitary brilliance. It is built through collective structure. Mutual funds exist as a testament to this principle—a financial engine fuelled by cooperation, not competition. And yet, despite their long-standing presence and remarkable accessibility, the fundamental nature of mutual funds is still poorly understood. They are often seen as passive or generic, lacking the intrigue of direct stock ownership or the allure of higher-stakes trading. But this perception misses the essence of what mutual funds *are*: dynamic, cooperative vehicles that harness the power of shared risk and shared return to create a system where the individual investor is no longer alone.

Imagine for a moment an economic co-operative—neighbours pooling money to build something none could afford individually: a well, a windmill, a barn. Each person contributes according to their ability, and each benefits according to their share. This basic logic is the foundation of mutual fund investing. Dozens, hundreds, even thousands of investors pool their capital into a single fund. That fund, guided by a defined investment objective, is then managed by professionals who deploy the collective capital into a portfolio of securities: equities, bonds, or a combination thereof. Each investor owns units in the fund proportional to their contribution, and as the fund grows in value—through dividends, interest, or capital gains—so too does the value of each unit.

This design is not incidental. It solves several problems at once. It provides access to markets that would otherwise be inaccessible to small investors. It enables diversification across sectors and asset classes—something prohibitively expensive to replicate with individual stock purchases. And perhaps most importantly, it redistributes the emotional weight of investing. When you invest through a mutual fund, you are not carrying the burden of decision-making alone. You are part of a guided system. The highs and lows are shared. The volatility is diffused. The structure absorbs panic before it becomes action.

The idea of shared risk is often misunderstood. Risk-sharing does not eliminate risk—it repositions it. In a mutual fund, your exposure is not concentrated in a few individual companies or market bets. It is spread across a basket of investments selected according to the fund's strategy. If one company underperforms, others may offset the decline. The individual is insulated from the extremes. This principle is critical not just mathematically, but psychologically. Investors are more likely to stay invested when their portfolios are buffered against catastrophic loss. Mutual funds offer this psychological safety net, and in doing so, protect investors from their own worst instincts.

Contrast this with the model of individual stock picking. Here, the investor must identify promising companies, monitor news and earnings, respond to market shifts, and—crucially—know when to sell. Each decision point introduces the possibility of error, and those errors often cluster in stressful conditions. Behavioural finance research has shown time and again that individual investors tend to buy high and sell low, chasing performance or fleeing volatility. This is not a failure of intelligence; it is a predictable pattern rooted in human psychology. Mutual funds, by design, reduce the frequency and necessity of such decisions. They channel investment activity through strategy rather than emotion.

To extend the metaphor further, think of mutual funds as a kind of guided group hike. You could attempt the same mountain alone—plotting your route, gauging the weather, managing your provisions. But unless you are an expert, the risks are high. A guided hike doesn't guarantee success, but it offers structure, support, and a significantly higher chance of completion. You walk not faster, but steadier. You are less likely to be thrown off course by a sudden storm or moment of fatigue. You move forward because the system keeps you in motion.

This does not mean that mutual funds are impersonal or static. On the contrary, they are highly responsive vehicles. The fund manager or management team monitors the portfolio daily, adjusting holdings in response to market dynamics, interest rate changes, earnings reports, or economic trends—always within the parameters set out in the fund's mandate. For example, a large-cap equity fund might reallocate from overvalued tech stocks to undervalued industrials if conditions warrant. A debt fund might shift from corporate bonds to sovereign instruments in response to a tightening credit environment. The investor does not have to make these adjustments; they are built into the system. This is not a removal of responsibility—it is a delegation to expertise.

And this delegation is scalable. A young professional contributing £200 a month to a mutual fund receives access to the same expertise, risk management, and research infrastructure as a high-net-worth investor contributing £200,000. The returns are proportional, but the structure is identical. This is where mutual funds demonstrate not just efficiency, but *equality of process*. They do not require sophistication, only participation. They do not reward bravado, only consistency.

Still, no structure is immune to distortion. The mutual fund industry—like any other—has its incentives, blind spots, and commercial pressures. Some funds carry hidden fees, excessive churn, or convoluted strategies designed more for marketing than performance. This is why clarity matters. It is not enough to understand that mutual funds pool resources. One must understand *how* they operate, *who* is making decisions, *what* the fees are, and *why* a particular fund exists. But these questions, once asked, are answerable. A mutual fund is not a black box. It is a public, regulated entity with clear documentation, published holdings, and legally mandated disclosures. Its transparency is a feature, not a flaw.

What this means for the individual investor is profound. You no longer need to rely on prediction, intuition, or media narratives. You can select a fund with a clear objective—growth, income, preservation—and align it with your own goals. You can automate contributions, ignore daily market fluctuations, and return your focus to your work, your family, your life. The fund works in the background, compounding not just your money, but your peace of mind.

This is not a retreat from responsibility. It is a deeper form of it. By choosing mutual funds, you are acknowledging that the best use of your energy is not constant surveillance of the market, but consistent alignment with a structure designed for long-term growth. You are respecting the complexity of markets by engaging with them in a way that is sustainable, repeatable, and scaled to your reality.

The collective nature of mutual funds is not merely a convenience. It is a philosophical commitment. It says that wealth-building is not just for those with time, access, or advanced knowledge. It is for anyone willing to participate in a system designed to amplify small actions over time. It replaces the illusion of control with the reality of structure. It makes investing accessible not by dumbing it down, but by designing it around real human behaviour.

Ultimately, the genius of mutual funds is not that they promise extraordinary returns. It is that they make *ordinary returns extraordinarily accessible.* They provide a mechanism through which the everyday investor can engage with the power of markets without becoming consumed by them. They allow you to stop performing as an investor and start behaving like one. And that behavioural shift—from sporadic attention to sustained participation—is where true financial progress begins. Mutual funds don't remove risk. But they reposition it in a way that is intelligible, manageable, and, for many, finally *liveable.* That is their power. That is their purpose. And that is why they matter.

Inside the Black Box: How a Fund Works

It is surprisingly common for people to invest in mutual funds without ever quite understanding what they are participating in. They contribute money each month, perhaps even glance at performance reports or Net Asset Value updates, yet remain largely in the dark about what actually takes place after that money leaves their bank account. Mutual funds, for all their accessibility, are often perceived as opaque—something closer to financial alchemy than transparent mechanism. But they are not a black box. When well-constructed and properly understood, a mutual fund is a logical, transparent system that converts individual contributions into collective opportunity, and distributes outcomes based on proportionate ownership. There is no mystery, no magic—just a tightly regulated, highly engineered structure designed to work on your behalf.

To demystify a mutual fund, begin with a simple premise: it is not an object, but a process. When you invest in a mutual fund, you are not buying shares in a single company, nor are you placing a bet on a particular sector or trend. You are purchasing units in a professionally managed portfolio—a pool of assets that evolves according to a defined investment objective. These assets can include equities, bonds, money market instruments, or a blend of all three. The type of securities the fund invests in depends entirely on its category and mandate: equity funds pursue growth by investing primarily in stocks, debt funds prioritise stability and income through fixed-income securities, and hybrid funds attempt to balance both.

Once your capital enters this pool, it becomes indistinguishable from the rest. You do not own specific stocks or bonds directly; instead, you own a claim on the fund itself, represented by units. The value of those units fluctuates based on the performance of the underlying assets. This value is expressed through the Net Asset Value (NAV), calculated daily by dividing the total value of the fund's assets (after subtracting liabilities) by the number of outstanding units. It is this NAV that determines whether your investment has grown or contracted on any given day.

The engine behind this system is the fund management team, often led by a designated fund manager. This individual or team operates under the guidance of the fund's prospectus—a legally binding document that outlines the fund's purpose, investment strategy, risk parameters, and operational framework. If the fund is actively managed, the manager makes deliberate decisions about which securities to buy, hold, or sell, using financial analysis, sector research, and economic forecasts. In a passive fund, such as an index fund, the manager's role is primarily operational—ensuring the fund's holdings mirror a specific market index as closely and cost-effectively as possible.

Critically, fund managers are not unconstrained. Their actions are scrutinised through internal risk committees, compliance officers, and external regulators. In the UK, for instance, mutual funds are governed by the Financial Conduct Authority (FCA), which imposes strict disclosure and conduct standards. This ecosystem of checks and balances is designed to ensure that fund management does not become an exercise in speculation, but remains anchored in fiduciary responsibility.

What happens when the fund earns income? Depending on the assets held, this income might take the form of dividends from equities, interest from bonds, or realised capital gains from the sale of profitable securities. These earnings are either distributed to investors in the form of payouts (in an income or dividend plan) or reinvested within the fund (in a growth plan), increasing the NAV and, by extension, the value of each unit held. You do not receive these earnings as isolated transactions; rather, they are embedded in the evolution of your investment's value. Over time, it is this reinvestment—especially when compounded—that becomes the engine of wealth creation.

But return generation is only one side of the equation. Cost control is the other. Every mutual fund charges fees to cover operational and management expenses. These are bundled into the expense ratio—a percentage deducted from the fund's assets annually. For example, if you invest in a fund with an expense ratio of 1.5%, and the fund grows by 8% in a year, your actual return before tax is effectively 6.5%. The difference may seem small, but over years or decades, it compounds. For this reason, understanding how fees are structured is not a peripheral concern—it is a core determinant of long term performance.

Different funds incur different types of costs. Actively managed funds tend to have higher expense ratios due to the resources required for research and discretionary decision-making. Passive funds are typically cheaper, as they follow a rules-based model that minimises overhead. Beyond the expense ratio, some funds impose entry loads (fees at the time of purchase) or exit loads (penalties for early withdrawal). These are less common today, especially in well-regulated markets, but their existence is a reminder that not all mutual funds are created equal. Some are designed with investor outcomes in mind; others with sales incentives.

So, how do you—as an investor—actually make money? There are three primary ways: through capital appreciation (NAV increases over time), through periodic distributions (dividends or interest payouts), and, in some cases, through tax advantages associated with long-term holding or specific fund categories. Importantly, returns are not guaranteed. Mutual funds, like any market-linked investment, are exposed to volatility. Their safety lies not in insulation from market forces, but in the way they manage those forces—through diversification, expert oversight, and disciplined strategy.

What distinguishes a mutual fund from speculative investing is not the absence of risk, but the intelligent handling of it. The fund structure reduces idiosyncratic risk by spreading exposure across multiple assets. It reduces emotional risk by outsourcing decisions to professionals. It reduces liquidity risk by allowing investors to enter or exit on any business day (in the case of open-ended funds). And it reduces timing risk when paired with systematic investment—monthly contributions that flatten the impact of market fluctuations through cost averaging.

The transparency of mutual funds is another often-overlooked advantage. While individual stocks or private investments can become opaque—subject to insider dynamics, selective disclosures, or erratic governance—mutual funds are required to publish detailed fact sheets, monthly portfolio disclosures, annual reports, and performance benchmarks. These documents are not mere formalities. They provide real-time visibility into where your money is invested, how it is being managed, and how it has performed relative to its stated goals. For the conscientious investor, this transparency is not only comforting—it is empowering.

Yet, despite all this clarity, the psychological hurdle remains. Many people still perceive mutual funds as inaccessible or mysterious. Part of the reason is cultural: investing is often presented as something reserved for the savvy, the well-read, or the financially fearless. But this assumption ignores the way mutual funds have been designed to function. Their structure does not demand expertise—it enables *participation.* The mutual fund, in its ideal form, is not a product for the few. It is a platform for the many.

Understanding how a fund works is the first step toward demystifying investing. It allows the investor to shift from a reactive mindset—hoping, guessing, fearing—to a proactive one rooted in trust and strategy. When you grasp the process, you stop viewing market movements as threats. You start seeing your investment as a system in motion—one guided not by your momentary opinions, but by a framework built for the long term.

This understanding also resets expectations. Mutual funds are not vehicles for instant wealth. They are not designed to "beat the market" through brilliance or timing. They are built to harness the market's potential over time, efficiently and accessibly. Their strength lies in compounding, not charisma. Their utility lies in habit, not heroics.

By unpacking what happens behind the scenes—who manages your money, how decisions are made, where returns come from, and what costs are involved—you take a step out of passivity. You no longer hand over your capital to a mysterious machine. You become a participant in a process. And once you understand that process, investing no longer feels like a gamble. It feels like something altogether more stable, more rational, and—ultimately—more human.

Why Funds Beat Individual Stock Picking for Most People

The enduring romance of stock picking rests on an alluring idea: that with enough insight, intuition, or research, one can consistently find undervalued gems, buy them early, and watch them soar. This idea is reinforced by media stories of legendary investors, by popular investing apps that offer sleek charts and real-time updates, and by a cultural bias that celebrates the lone strategist triumphing through intellect and courage. But for most investors, most of the time, this approach doesn't just underperform—it undermines their financial future. The data are unequivocal: *fund investing, particularly through diversified mutual or index funds, outperforms individual stock picking for the overwhelming majority of people.* The reasons are not only mathematical—they are psychological, structural, and deeply behavioural.

To understand why, we must first confront an uncomfortable truth: markets are highly efficient. This insight lies at the heart of modern portfolio theory, and has been validated by decades of empirical research, including the work of Nobel laureates such as Eugene

Fama and Harry Markowitz. Fama's Efficient Market Hypothesis (EMH), awarded the Nobel Prize in Economic Sciences in 2013, posits that all available information is already reflected in stock prices. What this means practically is that it is extremely difficult—if not impossible—for an individual investor to consistently outperform the market through active stock selection. Every advantage you believe you have is likely already priced in.

Of course, the EMH has been debated, revised, and challenged—particularly by behavioural economists such as Daniel Kahneman and Richard Thaler, who have shown that markets are not perfectly rational. But even these critics do not argue that individuals can reliably pick winning stocks. On the contrary, they highlight how *human investors routinely make systematic errors in judgement.* Overconfidence, confirmation bias, loss aversion, and herding behaviour distort rational decision-making and lead to poor outcomes over time. Stock picking is not just hard—it's *rigged against your psychology.*

One of the clearest demonstrations of this comes from DALBAR, a US-based financial research firm that has for decades tracked investor behaviour. Their annual reports consistently show that the average investor earns far less than the average mutual fund return. Why? Because of poor timing—buying high in exuberant markets and selling low in panicked downturns. These behavioural missteps erode returns far more aggressively than fees or market volatility ever could. The implication is blunt: *the investor is often their own worst enemy.*

Now consider the alternative: investing through mutual funds, particularly well-constructed, diversified equity or index funds. These instruments are not designed to beat the market—they are designed to *capture* it. Instead of making bets on individual companies, fund managers (or algorithms, in the case of index funds) allocate capital across dozens, hundreds, or even thousands of stocks. The aim is not outperformance through brilliance, but performance through breadth. The result is a smoother, more predictable exposure to long-term market growth.

This difference in approach—concentration versus diversification—is more than a technical distinction. It fundamentally reshapes risk. Individual stocks carry idiosyncratic risk: the chance that something specific to that company (a scandal, a failed product, a regulatory issue) could cause a sudden collapse in value. Diversified funds, by contrast, dilute this risk by spreading exposure. If one company falters, others in the portfolio may offset the decline. This *risk reduction through statistical correlation* is one of the most robust findings in finance, and underpins Markowitz's Nobel Prize-winning work on portfolio theory.

But diversification isn't just about mathematics. It is about behaviour. When investors hold a handful of stocks, they tend to monitor them obsessively, reacting to news stories, quarterly earnings reports, and even social media trends. This hyper-attention leads to impulsive trading and emotional whiplash. Diversified fund investors, by contrast, are more likely to stay invested. They know the performance of any single company matters less than the overall market trajectory. This detachment from micro-level volatility fosters discipline—a trait far more predictive of investment success than intellect.

Another overlooked advantage of mutual funds is cost efficiency. While some actively managed funds can be expensive, passive index funds often charge as little as 0.1% annually. Compare this to the hidden costs of stock picking: trading commissions (though reduced in many platforms), capital gains taxes from frequent selling, and the opportunity cost of idle cash waiting for the "right" moment. Over decades, these small frictions quietly siphon away returns. Funds, particularly those designed for long-term holding, minimise this drag through scale, automation, and tax efficiency.

Sceptics may point to the occasional investor who strikes gold with a single stock. And yes, these stories exist—early Amazon investors, those who backed Apple in the 1990s, or Tesla bulls who held through its volatility. But these are statistical outliers. They are no more replicable than lottery wins. Survivorship bias ensures we hear about the winners, not the countless others who bet big on the wrong company, mistimed their entry or exit, or held on too long. Building a portfolio on anecdotes is not a strategy. It's a gamble.

There is also the question of time. Stock picking demands research—deep analysis of financials, competitive positioning, macroeconomic factors, and management quality. Even professionals with access to proprietary data, teams of analysts, and advanced models struggle to outperform. For the average individual with a full-time job, family responsibilities, and limited bandwidth, the idea of constructing and maintaining a balanced stock portfolio is not just impractical—it is hubris. Funds allow you to bypass this complexity entirely. You don't have to be the expert. You just have to *participate in the system.*

Consider the case of two investors. Sarah spends hours each month researching stocks, constructing her own portfolio of ten companies. She reads earnings reports, follows market commentary, and adjusts her holdings quarterly. Meanwhile, James automates a monthly SIP into a low-cost index fund that tracks the FTSE All-World Index. He rarely checks his account. Ten years later, despite all her effort, Sarah's portfolio has underperformed James's—largely due to a few poor decisions and higher costs. James, while less engaged, allowed compounding and diversification to do their work. His result isn't luck. It's structural advantage.

Critically, none of this is an argument against engagement or education. Understanding the markets, learning how businesses work, and developing financial literacy are all valuable pursuits. But they are different from the act of placing concentrated bets on individual companies. Fund investing does not require ignorance. It simply recognises that *humility, consistency, and structure beat intensity, ego, and instinct.*

The psychological payoff is also worth noting. Investors who use mutual funds report lower stress, greater confidence, and a stronger sense of financial progress. Because the system is automated and diversified, they experience fewer decision points—and thus fewer chances to sabotage themselves. Investing ceases to be a source of anxiety and becomes a routine, almost invisible part of their lives. This emotional stability compounds just as powerfully as interest. It frees mental bandwidth and reinforces positive behaviours.

The debate between stock picking and fund investing is, at its heart, a question of design. One model relies on the investor's ongoing effort, insight, and composure. The other relies on systems that incorporate diversification, professional management, and behavioural protection. One is fragile and dependent on execution. The other is resilient by design. For most people—for people with full lives, competing demands, and limited desire to track markets daily—the answer is not even close.

Mutual funds are not a compromise. They are an optimisation of human limitations. They recognise that the most dangerous variable in investing is not the market—it's the investor. And they are built to protect us from ourselves. Not through restriction, but through intelligent structure.

Ultimately, the choice between picking stocks and using funds is not about belief in markets. It is about belief in *process*. Do you trust a system built on evidence, scale, and collective intelligence? Or do you trust your ability to outwit it, consistently, under pressure, over decades? The difference is not merely philosophical. It is measurable—in returns, in risk, in time, and in peace of mind. For most investors, the decision is not whether they can win the game. It's whether they should be playing it at all.

Fees, Fund Houses, and Hidden Traps

When most investors think about returns, they think in percentages—8% average annual growth, 10% long-term equity returns, 6% conservative expectations. But these numbers, quoted without scrutiny, often miss one of the most critical variables in the compounding equation: cost. In mutual fund investing, it is not the *headline* return that builds wealth—it is the *net* return after fees. And this difference, seemingly marginal in a single year, becomes decisive over decades. A fund that earns 9% but costs 2% does not merely underperform a fund earning 8% with a 0.2% fee. Over time, the compounding effect of lower costs far outstrips most differences in active management performance. Yet this fact remains underappreciated—even among otherwise well-informed investors.

The financial industry, like any other, is driven by incentives. Asset managers, brokers, platforms, and advisers all exist within a commercial ecosystem where revenue must be generated. This is neither surprising nor inherently unethical. But it means that fees, commissions, and embedded costs are not simply a footnote—they are central to how the investment product is structured and sold. Understanding them is not technical nitpicking. It is a form of self-protection.

The most fundamental fee to understand is the *expense ratio.* Expressed as an annual percentage of assets under management, this ratio covers the fund's operational costs: portfolio management, administration, legal and audit services, regulatory compliance, and marketing. It is deducted automatically, invisibly, from the fund's assets. You will not receive a bill; the fee reduces the Net Asset Value (NAV) of your units. A 1.5% expense ratio may sound modest. But over 30 years, it can reduce your total returns by tens—sometimes hundreds—of thousands in lost compounding.

This is particularly troubling when the fee is not justified by performance. Numerous studies, including longitudinal research from Morningstar and the SPIVA Scorecard series published by S&P Dow Jones Indices, have shown that higher-cost funds rarely outperform their cheaper peers on a risk-adjusted basis. In fact, expense ratio is one of the most reliable predictors of underperformance. Funds with the highest fees consistently lag their benchmarks, not because their managers are inept, but because the structural headwind of cost is difficult to overcome.

It is here that index funds reveal their core advantage. With expense ratios as low as 0.05% in some cases, they represent one of the most cost-efficient ways to access the equity or bond markets. They do not attempt to outperform; they simply aim to replicate the index. The lack of active management dramatically reduces costs, and over time, this difference compounds powerfully. For investors focused on long-term growth, this is not a minor detail—it is a strategic foundation.

Yet even within actively managed funds, some fees are justifiable. Skilled fund managers operating in specialised or less efficient markets—such as small-cap equities or emerging markets—may warrant higher fees due to the research intensity required. But this justification must be backed by *consistent, benchmark-beating performance net of fees* across multiple market cycles. If it's not, the premium is simply erosion.

Beyond the expense ratio, investors must contend with *loads*. An *entry load* (or front-end load) is a commission paid when purchasing a fund. For example, a 5% entry load on a £10,000 investment means only £9,500 is actually invested. The remainder compensates the distributor or intermediary. *Exit loads* penalise investors who withdraw funds within a specified holding period, often ranging from 1% to 2%. While regulatory reforms have reduced the prevalence of loads in many jurisdictions, they still appear in legacy funds, less regulated markets, or within bundled insurance-investment products disguised as mutual funds.

Then there are *distribution commissions*—ongoing fees paid to financial advisers or platforms for recommending or maintaining the fund in your portfolio. These are typically built into the expense ratio under a category known as "12b-1 fees" in the U.S. or "trail commissions" elsewhere. The ethical problem is not that advisers are paid. It's that the investor often does not know *how much*, or whether the adviser's recommendation is influenced more by commission than suitability.

The next trap is more subtle: *fund house marketing tactics*. Asset management companies compete not just on returns or reputation, but on visibility. Glossy brochures, sponsored articles, and performance ads touting "#1 fund in category" status are not evidence of superior investment strategy—they are branding exercises. Even more misleading are star ratings and past-performance rankings that do not account for survivorship bias, cherry-picked time periods, or shifts in fund management.

This is where behavioural bias meets commercial strategy. Investors are drawn to funds with recent outperformance, only to switch again when the inevitable reversion to the mean occurs. This cycle of performance-chasing, fuelled by slick marketing, benefits fund houses through increased turnover and higher fee collection—but typically leaves investors worse off. The DALBAR studies repeatedly show that investor returns lag *fund* returns, largely due to this timing mismatch.

Transparency is further muddied by fund complexity. Many large fund houses offer dozens—sometimes hundreds—of products with overlapping mandates. A single provider might offer five different large-cap funds, each with nuanced differences in strategy, management style, or fee structure. Without clear guidance or disclosure, the average investor may select a fund based on brand familiarity or headline return, unaware that a lower-cost, better-aligned option from the same provider is available.

A more technical trap involves *churn*—the frequent buying and selling of securities within the fund. High turnover generates trading costs, taxes, and slippage, all of which reduce returns. While these do not appear in the expense ratio, they represent a meaningful hidden cost, particularly in actively managed equity funds. A fund with a turnover rate of 100% or more is effectively reshuffling its portfolio every year. This may be justified in niche strategies, but in most cases, it reflects either short-termism or a misguided attempt to "add value."

Investors must also be wary of "closet indexers"—actively managed funds that charge high fees but closely mimic a benchmark index in their holdings. These funds offer little active insight while charging as though they do. They are the worst of both worlds: high cost, low differentiation. Identifying them requires reviewing fund holdings and comparing them to the index, a task few retail investors perform without guidance.

Then there's the issue of tax inefficiency. Mutual funds, particularly in markets without tax-sheltered wrappers like ISAs or SIPPs, can expose investors to capital gains distributions triggered by internal portfolio changes. In some jurisdictions, even if the investor does not sell their fund units, they may be liable for gains realised within the fund. This is why tax-aware investing—choosing low-turnover funds, growth plans over dividend payouts, or using tax-advantaged accounts—is not merely tactical, but essential.

So what can an investor do to avoid these traps without becoming a forensic analyst? Begin by demanding transparency. Every fund must disclose its expense ratio, turnover rate, holdings, and historical performance relative to a benchmark. Compare not just the returns, but the *consistency* of those returns after costs. Understand the difference between direct and regular plans if investing through a platform. Ask whether your adviser is fee-only or commission-based. If they cannot answer clearly, walk away.

Above all, adopt a sceptical stance toward promises of outperformance. In investing, *structure beats story.* A low-cost, diversified fund aligned with your time horizon and risk tolerance will almost always outperform a higher-cost fund picked for recent returns or marketing polish. Fees may seem like background noise in bullish markets, but over decades, they are one of the most reliable indicators of who builds real wealth—and who subsidises someone else's margins.

The financial system will not simplify itself for your benefit. Complexity often serves those who design it. But with even a modest level of scrutiny, the investor can reclaim agency. You do not need to master every ratio or footnote. You simply need to know what to ask, what to notice, and what to avoid. Once you strip away the marketing language and interrogate the fee structure, mutual funds stop being opaque products and start becoming what they were designed to be: *efficient vehicles for collective growth*. But that efficiency depends on your ability to keep more of what you earn. And that begins by understanding what's being taken away—quietly, annually, and entirely avoidably.

Chapter 3
Meet the Fund Family

Many people hear "mutual fund" and imagine a singular, monolithic product—a bland financial placeholder, vaguely tethered to the stock market. That perception, however, is both simplistic and misleading. Mutual funds are not a single vehicle but a diverse ecosystem. Just as homes vary in purpose—some built for growth, others for shelter, some for flexibility—so too do different mutual funds serve distinct roles within a portfolio. Understanding these roles is not a mere academic exercise; it forms the bedrock of a resilient, personalised investment strategy.

This chapter invites a closer look at the architecture of mutual funds—not only how they function, but what they represent in their myriad forms and for what objectives they are designed. Once we move beyond the abstract notion of "investing in a fund," we encounter a spectrum of vehicles tailored to particular goals, timelines, and temperaments. The fund family is less a collection of options than a set of strategic tools. Each has an optimal context and inherent trade-offs, and knowing these is essential.

At the centre of most portfolios lies the equity fund—the engine of long-term growth. Equity funds invest in shares of publicly listed companies, providing exposure to the productive capacity of businesses across sectors and geographies. But not all equity funds are identical. Some focus on large-cap firms—financial skyscrapers: stable, slow-growing, reliable. Others target mid-cap companies, akin to suburban developments: expanding, evolving, with moderate volatility. Small-cap funds pursue startups or niche players, cabins in the woods: high potential, high uncertainty. Selecting among these is less about memorising risk tables and more about aligning with your time horizon, temperament, and investment philosophy.

At the other end of the spectrum are debt funds—vehicles designed for stability. Where equity funds chase growth, debt funds are essentially contracts for repayment. They lend to governments, corporations, or other entities in exchange for interest. Their appeal lies in predictability. Often, they act as ballast within a portfolio, countering market turbulence with steady, if modest, returns. Yet even debt funds contain nuance. Government-bond funds are low-risk but yield little; corporate-bond funds offer higher returns but carry credit risk; dynamic-duration funds adjust exposure in line with interest-rate expectations, requiring a more sophisticated understanding of macroeconomics. To treat all debt funds as interchangeable is to miss the artistry in their deployment—as shock absorbers, income streams, or tactical instruments during market stress.

Bridging these poles are hybrid, or balanced, funds—an effort to combine equity and debt within a single vehicle. Hybrids offer diversified exposure, with stock-to-bond ratios defined by the fund's mandate. For beginners, they provide a gentle entry into markets, testing the waters without full exposure to volatility. For seasoned investors, they present tactical flexibility: maintaining exposure while modulating risk. Yet hybrids are not without pitfalls. Their blended nature can obscure underlying exposures, leading to misjudged volatility. Choosing them demands deliberate intention, not compromise.

Specialist funds, including thematic and sectoral products, concentrate investments in a single industry, trend, or concept—technology, ESG, infrastructure, or even emerging domains like artificial intelligence or space exploration. The potential rewards are matched by amplified risk. Sectoral funds are like eggs in a basket crafted from one material: any crack—regulatory, consumer, or geopolitical—can imperil the whole allocation. They are not portfolio anchors but accent pieces, requiring clarity of purpose, disciplined allocation, and acceptance of their speculative character.

Together, these categories form the fund family—but this is more than taxonomy; it is a call to intentionality. Each fund type reflects a particular relationship to uncertainty, time, and temperament. Equity demands patience and belief in capitalism's arc; debt appeals to predictability and steady income; hybrids suit pragmatists seeking balance; thematic funds attract the bold or curious. No orientation is inherently superior; suitability depends on your goals, psychology, and context.

This chapter aims to cultivate discernment, not rote knowledge. The objective is to see fund types as manifestations of underlying investment logic. Why might someone in their twenties favour equity despite market uncertainty? Why might a retiree prefer laddered debt over cash holdings? Why might a mid-career professional select a hybrid rather than managing individual assets? These are strategic questions, blending risk, reward, and personal responsibility.

We will also explore how fund houses design, differentiate, and market these products. Not all equity funds follow the same strategy; not all debt funds share credit profiles. The abundance of options enables precision but also risks confusion or misalignment. Effective navigation demands scrutiny beyond labels: asset allocation, management style, historical volatility, expense ratios, and philosophical approach. The goal is not perfection, but informed decision-making.

This chapter builds on a foundational premise: one need not be a financial prodigy to invest wisely—but attention to what matters is indispensable. Fund type is one such element. It signals how your money is intended to behave in the world. And since money represents your time, labour, and aspirations, these choices are profoundly personal.

Analogies, critiques, and case studies throughout this chapter aim to convert theory into intuition. You will distinguish growth-focused equity funds from high-yield debt, understand which funds accelerate wealth and which stabilise it, and appreciate that diversification is not merely about asset classes, but aligning fund behaviour with life rhythm.

By the end, you should be able to assess any mutual fund within a coherent framework: its function, role, and fit with your needs, today and tomorrow. This clarity transforms investing from guesswork into craftsmanship. In a world saturated with financial noise, clarity itself is power.

The fund family is not abstract classification; it is the blueprint of your financial foundation. Understand its forms, recognise their uses, and you will be equipped to build something enduring—

resilient, intentional, and aligned with who you are and what you value.

Equity Funds: Growth with Volatility:

When people imagine investing for the long term, they're often picturing something vague: the market rising, wealth accumulating, maybe a graph trending upward in a slow but reassuring curve. What they're usually imagining—without naming it—is the power of equity mutual funds. These funds, which pool investor money to buy shares in publicly traded companies, are the backbone of most serious long-term investment strategies. Yet despite their central role, they remain misunderstood, often reduced to simplified categories or overshadowed by flashier financial instruments. To understand equity funds is to understand one of the most efficient, flexible, and time-tested ways to participate in economic growth without needing to master the complexity of individual stock picking.

Equity mutual funds are designed for growth. That much is clear. But what makes them powerful isn't just the possibility of high returns—it's how they translate the dynamism of capitalism into a structured, diversified, and professionally managed vehicle. Unlike holding individual stocks, where the fate of your capital might rest on the next earnings call or a CEO's impulsive decision, equity funds spread your risk across many companies, industries, and sometimes even geographies. The result is *exposure to opportunity without the burden of constant vigilance.* It's a strategy built not on prediction, but participation.

The core appeal of equity funds lies in this balance: they offer access to long-term capital appreciation while managing the downside risks that come with individual equities. They are not without volatility, but the volatility they carry is often a feature, not a flaw. Over time, what appears as short-term fluctuation is often reabsorbed into upward momentum—provided the investor resists the temptation to interfere. This is the behavioural edge of equity fund investing: it rewards patience over precision.

To grasp the range of equity mutual funds, it's useful to consider them not as a single investment type, but as a spectrum of strategies differentiated by market capitalisation—large-cap, mid-cap, and small-cap funds. Each reflects a different phase of corporate maturity and a different kind of risk-return profile. A useful way to internalise this is through a real-world analogy: think of building different types of homes.

Large-cap equity funds are like urban skyscrapers. They are built by established players, backed by strong foundations, and designed for resilience. These funds invest in the biggest, most stable companies—blue chips with consistent earnings, global operations, and institutional confidence. Think of firms like Unilever, Nestlé, or Microsoft. Their growth may be slower, but it's steady. Their volatility may be lower, but so is the chance of explosive gain. Large-cap funds provide structural stability—ideal for those who want reliable long-term growth with less emotional turbulence.

Mid-cap funds are more akin to well-planned suburban developments—still under construction, but with blueprints for scale. These funds target companies that have moved past the volatile early phase but haven't yet saturated their markets. They tend to be more agile, more innovative, and, in many cases, more exposed to regional or emerging trends. The trade-off is that they can be more vulnerable during downturns. Yet historically, mid-cap funds have often outperformed both large- and small-cap categories over certain time horizons, offering a compelling balance between risk and reward.

Then there are small-cap equity funds—the equivalent of bespoke, experimental homes built in frontier territories. These funds invest in relatively new or niche companies with high growth potential but limited track records. The promise here is asymmetry: small amounts invested can yield disproportionately large returns—*if* the companies succeed. But the risk of failure is real and present. Small-cap funds are not for the faint-hearted. They are better suited to those with longer time horizons, a higher risk appetite, and the ability to tolerate significant interim volatility without abandoning ship.

Each of these fund types has its place in a well-constructed portfolio. The question is not which one is "best," but which combination is most aligned with your financial goals, time horizon, and capacity for uncertainty. A young investor with decades ahead might lean heavily into small- and mid-cap funds, riding out the turbulence for higher long-term returns. A retiree might prefer the consistency of large-cap holdings, even if it means sacrificing some upside. A professional in mid-career might blend all three, seeking to balance stability with growth.

What's essential to understand is that *growth with volatility is not a flaw of equity funds— it is their character.* Attempting to chase performance by switching between fund types, entering and exiting based on market noise, is where most investors go wrong. Study after study shows that investor returns are often lower than fund returns—not because the funds underperformed, but because the investors didn't stay invested. This behaviour gap is well documented by firms like Morningstar, which routinely report that investor timing decisions erode potential gains.

Equity mutual funds offer a behavioural advantage precisely because they create a psychological buffer. By pooling capital with others and delegating decision-making to professional fund managers, investors insulate themselves from their own worst instincts. They are less likely to panic, less likely to overreact, and more likely to stay the course—especially when investing through Systematic Investment Plans (SIPs) that automate contributions and reduce decision fatigue.

Another underappreciated strength of equity funds is their embedded research discipline. Unlike retail investors who rely on headlines or gut feelings, fund managers are required to perform in-depth due diligence. They evaluate financials, leadership quality, competitive position, and macroeconomic trends. While no fund manager has a crystal ball, the structural process by which equities are selected in most funds is far more rigorous than the average do-it-yourself investor's methods. This doesn't guarantee outperformance, but it significantly increases the probability of avoiding catastrophic missteps—especially in diversified, passively managed index equity funds.

For many readers, the most valuable shift is not just in understanding what equity funds are, but *how to think about them.* They are not stock substitutes, nor are they passive parking spots for money. They are mechanisms for participating in human ingenuity at scale. When you invest in an equity fund, you are, in essence, placing capital in the hands of businesses solving real-world problems, innovating, and competing in dynamic markets. This is capitalism at its most constructive—not as speculation, but as contribution.

Yet this must come with a note of humility. Past performance is not a predictor of future results, and markets are shaped by uncertainty as much as data. Equity funds, for all their strengths, are not immune to downturns. What protects the long-term investor is not the cleverness of the fund, but the consistency of their own behaviour. Staying invested through downturns, resisting the temptation to exit during drawdowns, and allowing time to do its compounding work—that is the edge that equity fund investors carry.

A deeper understanding of equity mutual funds also dispels the illusion of control that often haunts retail investors. In an attempt to "beat the market," many waste hours monitoring stocks, reacting to news, and endlessly rebalancing. But most wealth creation does not come from relentless tweaking. It comes from strategic alignment followed by disciplined inaction. This is the subtle brilliance of equity funds: they allow you to *decide once, and benefit many times*, provided you choose well and trust the process.

In this chapter, we will go further into each of these fund categories—large-cap, mid-cap, and small-cap—examining their construction, historical performance patterns, risk factors, and common misconceptions. We will also explore the role they play in a diversified portfolio, how to mix them effectively, and what mistakes to avoid when allocating across them. By the end of this section, the reader will not just understand equity mutual funds—they will know how to use them intentionally.

If you are looking for wealth that builds over decades rather than weeks, that survives cycles rather than chases them, and that rewards steadiness over speculation, then equity funds deserve your close attention. They are not a magic bullet, but they are a powerful tool—

and in the right hands, with the right expectations, they are often enough.

Debt Funds: Stability Over Speed:

It is a curious paradox of modern investing that the greatest attention often flows toward the assets with the loudest fluctuations—stocks that surge or plummet, funds that outperform benchmarks by fractions of a percent, currencies that wobble on headlines. In this whirlwind of financial chatter, it is easy to overlook a quieter, steadier instrument: the debt mutual fund. While equity funds get the spotlight for their growth potential, debt funds occupy a less glamorous—but no less vital—corner of the investment landscape. Their function is not to dazzle, but to stabilise. Not to accelerate, but to absorb. And for many investors—especially the risk-averse, the income-focused, or the nearing-retirement—their contribution can be the difference between a fragile plan and a resilient one.

Debt mutual funds, at their essence, pool investor money to lend it out to governments, corporations, or financial institutions by purchasing fixed-income securities like bonds, treasury bills, or certificates of deposit. In return, these funds earn interest income, which is then passed on to the investor. They don't depend on bull markets, earnings surprises, or speculative trends. They rely on something more prosaic but equally powerful: *the obligation to repay*. This simple fact—that a bond is a contract, not a gamble—underpins the core appeal of debt funds.

To appreciate the role of debt funds, it's helpful to think of a portfolio not as a single monolithic vehicle, but as a multi-gear transmission. Equity funds might be the high gears—useful for acceleration—but no intelligent driver relies on those alone. Debt funds are the lower gears that provide traction on slippery terrain, stability on declines, and control when circumstances demand caution. In market downturns, when equity values are falling and investor sentiment is shaken, it is often the steady drip of income from debt funds that allows a portfolio to maintain balance, both mathematically and psychologically.

Yet despite their value, many retail investors misunderstand—or underestimate—these instruments. The reasons are not difficult to decipher. Debt funds lack the narrative drama that equity markets provide. There are no high-stakes quarterly earnings calls, no charismatic CEOs to follow, no soaring tech stock headlines. Instead, what you get is interest income, principal preservation, and modest but reliable growth. It is investing for those who prioritise *capital preservation over capital appreciation.* For those who understand that sometimes, staying still is a strategy.

This does not mean debt funds are risk-free. On the contrary, they involve distinct types of risk—interest rate risk, credit risk, and liquidity risk, to name the key ones. Interest rate risk refers to the inverse relationship between bond prices and interest rates. When rates rise, the value of existing bonds typically falls. Credit risk involves the possibility that a bond issuer might default, while liquidity risk captures the difficulty of selling a bond quickly without affecting its price. However, unlike equity risks—which are largely driven by sentiment, valuation, and macro shocks—debt risks are often measurable, foreseeable, and manageable through diversification and fund selection.

Different categories of debt funds cater to different appetites and time horizons. Liquid funds, for example, invest in ultra-short-term instruments and are designed for short holding periods—ideal for parking idle cash with slightly better returns than a savings account. Short-duration and corporate bond funds, by contrast, invest in high-quality papers with short to medium maturities, aiming for stability with reasonable yields. Gilt funds focus exclusively on government securities, offering safety at the expense of slightly higher interest rate sensitivity. Then there are credit risk funds, which deliberately take exposure to lower-rated corporate debt for the potential of higher returns—a category not for the faint-hearted and often misunderstood during market stress.

The diversity of these categories allows investors to construct an intelligent fixed-income layer within their portfolios—one that can be dialled up or down based on market conditions, personal income needs, and risk tolerance. For conservative investors, debt funds offer an alternative to fixed deposits—often with better post-tax returns and higher liquidity. For older investors, they provide income with lower volatility. For young investors, they act as a ballast—helping counterbalance more aggressive equity allocations and providing dry powder during corrections.

What makes debt mutual funds particularly powerful in the context of Indian households—and increasingly in global ones—is their potential to replace outdated savings behaviours. In many families, surplus cash sits in bank accounts earning below-inflation returns or is locked in fixed deposits with inflexible terms. Debt funds provide a middle ground: capital that is accessible, reasonably safe, and capable of growing quietly in the background. For example, a systematic transfer plan (STP) from a liquid fund into an equity fund allows investors to earn income while averaging into market risk. This kind of mechanism is only possible when the underlying instrument—like a liquid or ultra-short fund—is predictable and stable.

Tax efficiency also plays a role, though the landscape is shifting. While debt funds once enjoyed favourable long-term capital gains treatment, recent reforms have narrowed the advantage. Nevertheless, for investors in higher tax brackets, the potential for post-tax optimisation remains when compared with traditional bank products. The key, as always, is to align the investment with one's real-life cash flow and tax profile—not just to seek returns in the abstract.

Perhaps the most overlooked strength of debt funds is psychological. During equity drawdowns, it is the sight of stable, income-producing holdings that often prevents panic selling. Debt funds act as *emotional shock absorbers*, providing calm when the rest of the portfolio is under stress. For older investors drawing down from their assets, the predictability of returns is not just comforting—it is essential. A portfolio that relies too heavily on equities may show strong long-term returns on paper but could suffer from unsustainable volatility in practice, especially when withdrawals are involved. Debt funds mitigate this sequence risk, smoothing the experience of retirement spending.

Yet not all debt funds are created equal, and here the investor must be vigilant. The pursuit of marginally higher yields has led many funds into murky waters—taking on greater credit risk than advertised, extending durations subtly, or engaging in aggressive portfolio churning. The IL&FS crisis, the Franklin Templeton debt fund freeze, and other episodes have reminded investors that transparency and fund governance matter. It is not enough to chase the top-yielding debt fund on a comparison site. One must understand what lies beneath—what papers are being held, what credit assumptions are being made, how liquid the underlying instruments are, and how responsive the fund manager is to market shifts.

Fortunately, reputable fund houses often offer detailed monthly fact sheets, credit quality breakdowns, and duration metrics. A thoughtful investor can, with a bit of education, read these not as raw data, but as narratives. A low-duration fund with AAA-rated instruments tells one story: safety-first, income-stable. A credit risk fund with 30% in sub-AA papers tells another: ambition laced with fragility. The difference matters—not just in returns, but in sleep quality.

What debt funds ultimately teach is the value of restraint. They are the adult in the room when everything else is promising riches. They remind us that *wealth isn't only about maximising gain—it's about minimising regret.* That protecting what you have is as important as growing what you don't. That risk-adjusted returns—rather than raw performance—are what determine whether an investment strategy is truly sustainable.

For those constructing portfolios with care—whether for retirement, education, housing, or intergenerational wealth—debt funds offer the scaffolding. They don't shout. They don't spike. But they provide something rarer: the ability to breathe easy, knowing that part of your capital is working patiently, quietly, and responsibly.

In the chapters that follow, we will examine how to select the right kind of debt fund for your objectives, how to interpret their structure and disclosures, and how to balance them against your more aggressive holdings. By the end of this section, you will see that safety is not the opposite of ambition—it is the condition that allows it to endure.

Balanced & Hybrid Funds: The Best of Both Worlds?:

Risk and return are often framed as adversaries in personal finance—as though the only meaningful choice investors must make is whether to chase gains or protect capital. This false binary has deterred countless individuals from participating meaningfully in markets, convincing them that investing is either a bold, all-or-nothing game or something best left to experts. But within the broad landscape of mutual funds exists a nuanced alternative: the hybrid fund. Often described as the middle ground between equity and debt, hybrid or balanced funds challenge the notion that investors must choose between risk and safety. Properly understood, they offer something more sophisticated—a way to *modulate* exposure, not merely split it.

At a structural level, hybrid funds invest in both equity and fixed income securities, typically with a predefined allocation. Depending on the fund type—aggressive hybrid, conservative hybrid, dynamic asset allocation, or arbitrage—the mix may lean more toward stocks, bonds, or shift flexibly in response to market conditions. But it's not the ratio alone that makes them compelling. It's what that ratio *enables*: participation in equity upside without full exposure to its volatility, and income generation without sacrificing long-term growth. In effect, hybrid funds offer investors an opportunity to *test the waters of risk* without being submerged by it.

This is particularly powerful for first-time or anxious investors—those who are intellectually convinced of the need to invest but emotionally paralysed by market unpredictability. Imagine an individual in their mid-30s with a steady job, some savings in a fixed deposit, and a vague awareness that inflation is quietly eroding their purchasing power. They know they should invest, but the equity market feels like foreign terrain, full of jargon and peril. A hybrid fund, especially a balanced advantage fund with dynamic rebalancing, becomes a psychological bridge: a professionally managed vehicle that adapts to market conditions, maintains diversification, and crucially, dampens volatility.

One of the reasons this works is behavioural. Human psychology is notoriously poor at managing risk in the abstract. Investors may tolerate the *idea* of a 10% market correction but struggle emotionally when it affects their real money. Hybrid funds buffer this reaction. By holding debt instruments alongside equities, they reduce the magnitude of drawdowns during market stress. This doesn't eliminate the possibility of loss, but it blunts the sharp edges—helping investors stay the course instead of fleeing at the worst moment. The result is not just better short-term experience, but potentially *better long-term outcomes*, because consistency, not brilliance, compounds most effectively.

A particularly instructive case is the performance of aggressive hybrid funds during recent market cycles. Funds with a 65–80% equity allocation and the rest in debt weathered downturns more gracefully than pure equity funds, thanks to the cushion provided by fixed income. During recovery periods, they participated significantly in the upside—though not as much as fully equity-weighted portfolios. For many investors, this trade-off—reduced upside in exchange for lower downside volatility—is not a compromise, but a smart calibration. It aligns with real-world goals, where emotional sustainability and time in the market often matter more than outperforming a benchmark.

Hybrid funds also introduce a subtle but critical conceptual shift: the idea that asset allocation is not static, but responsive. Dynamic asset allocation funds, for instance, adjust their equity and debt exposure based on market valuations, interest rates, or volatility metrics. Rather than asking investors to predict market turns themselves—a notoriously unproductive endeavour—these funds institutionalise discipline. They move into equity when valuations are attractive, and shift toward debt when markets are overheated. It's a form of embedded counter-cyclicality that serves investors who lack either the time, skill, or temperament to make such calls independently.

This adaptability is where hybrid funds differentiate themselves most sharply from simple diversification. Traditional portfolios might hold separate equity and debt funds, leaving the investor to manage the rebalancing manually. In contrast, hybrid funds internalise that function. For example, a balanced advantage fund might shift from

80% equity to 40% equity over a few months based on valuation metrics like the price-to-book ratio or earnings yield gap. These adjustments aren't perfect, but they instil a logic of *systematic discipline* that often eludes individual investors.

Yet it's essential to be clear-eyed about limitations. Hybrid funds are not a panacea. Their flexibility can sometimes become opacity—particularly in dynamic or balanced advantage funds where the shifting allocations are complex or poorly disclosed. Not all funds follow a transparent model; some rely heavily on proprietary formulas or discretionary calls by fund managers, making it hard for the retail investor to understand what exactly they are buying. And in trying to deliver "the best of both worlds", some funds may end up underperforming pure-play equity or debt options during strong directional moves.

Another consideration is cost. Hybrid funds tend to have slightly higher expense ratios than their pure equity or debt counterparts, especially those employing dynamic strategies. Over long periods, these incremental fees can erode returns. The trade-off, again, is convenience and behavioural support—investors pay for professional rebalancing and volatility management. But the value of that trade-off must be judged individually, based on the investor's temperament and goals.

Taxation, too, introduces complexity. In jurisdictions like India, hybrid funds with more than 65% equity exposure are taxed as equity for capital gains purposes, offering a potential tax advantage over pure debt funds. However, this structure can tempt some fund houses to maintain equity exposure just above the threshold—even when market conditions don't justify it—to preserve the tax treatment. This underscores the importance of scrutinising not just the label, but the underlying strategy and historical behaviour of the fund.

Ultimately, hybrid funds represent a more *forgiving entry point* into the world of market-linked investing. They don't require the investor to have a strong view on equity versus debt, nor do they demand the emotional steel to withstand severe drawdowns unbuffered. They also allow investors to begin building experience with market-linked instruments in a context that prioritises stability as much as return. Over time, as investors become more comfortable, some may migrate to more targeted strategies. Others may find that a well-chosen hybrid fund meets their long-term needs fully—especially when paired with consistent contributions and periodic reviews.

What's critical is recognising that hybrid funds are not merely a blend of assets—they're a bridge between risk philosophies. For the young professional uncertain about equity, the retiree seeking some growth without endangering income, or the middle-aged saver trying to recalibrate after market losses, hybrid funds offer a practical, structured way to move forward. They respect the investor's uncertainty without capitulating to it. They accommodate caution without penalising ambition.

If mutual funds are to become tools of personal empowerment, not confusion, then hybrid funds may be the most accessible handle to grasp. They invite participation without demanding perfection. They soften the edges of volatility without eliminating growth. They manage risk not by avoiding it, but by *right-sizing* it. And in doing so, they turn hesitation into progress—one calibrated allocation at a time.

Thematic and Sectoral Funds: When Focus Becomes Risk:

There is a peculiar allure to precision in investing—the sense that if one can just identify *the right industry at the right time*, wealth creation becomes not only possible, but rapid. This belief fuels the enduring appeal of thematic and sectoral mutual funds. Unlike diversified equity funds that spread investments across industries, these specialised funds concentrate on a specific theme—such as artificial intelligence, infrastructure, ESG, or healthcare—or a single sector like banking, technology, or pharmaceuticals. At first glance, this appears deeply rational: after all, why scatter your bets when you believe you've identified the next breakout trend? But it is this very concentration—the narrowing of scope—that transforms thematic funds from potentially strategic instruments into dangerous speculative vehicles when misunderstood or misused.

To be clear, thematic and sectoral funds are not inherently flawed. When deployed with discernment, they can play a valuable role within a diversified portfolio. The problem arises when investors mistake *narrative coherence for investment certainty*. A compelling story—renewable energy is the future, India's infrastructure boom is imminent, tech is eating the world—can seduce investors into overexposure. But compelling stories are not a substitute for margin of safety. Nor do they immunise portfolios from cyclical downturns, regulatory setbacks, or shifting global dynamics. Sectoral funds magnify these risks by design. When an entire fund is tied to a single economic segment, the investor is no longer protected by diversification but entirely beholden to that segment's trajectory.

Consider the banking and financial services sector in India. In the post-2008 period, financial sector funds were among the top performers, buoyed by high credit growth, rising consumption, and regulatory support. This led many investors to overallocate, assuming past performance would persist. But in subsequent years—particularly during the non-performing asset crisis and the liquidity crunch of 2018—returns plummeted, and sectoral overexposure became a liability. The same pattern has played out globally in other industries: technology funds during the dot-com boom, energy funds during the oil supercycle, or real estate-linked investments prior to the 2008 crash. The lesson is not that these sectors lack merit, but that *timing and exposure matter profoundly when focus increases fragility*.

From a behavioural standpoint, thematic funds often tap into what psychologists call *narrative bias*. Investors feel reassured when a fund's purpose aligns with broader social, technological, or geopolitical trends they already believe in. If you are convinced that electric vehicles are the future, a fund exclusively focused on EV and battery companies may feel like an obvious choice. But this emotional validation masks an essential question: *what is already priced in?* Thematic funds often launch at the height of enthusiasm, when valuations in the target sector are already stretched. This creates a dangerous mismatch between investor expectations and return realities. Investors buy in after the narrative has matured, only to discover that future upside has been eroded by early enthusiasm.

There's also the issue of time horizon. Thematic and sectoral bets are, by definition, narrow in their exposure. This means they require *longer holding periods* to realise potential returns and to ride out sector-specific volatility. But most retail investors do not have the patience or understanding to weather prolonged underperformance. A fund that dips 25% while broader diversified funds hold steady creates anxiety. Investors redeem early, locking in losses and reinforcing a cycle of fear and regret. This is especially risky in thematic funds built around emerging ideas, where business models, regulations, and adoption timelines are still evolving. Without a clear thesis and disciplined allocation, what starts as strategic exposure often devolves into expensive speculation.

This does not mean these funds have no place in a rational investment framework. In fact, for experienced investors or those with specific convictions supported by rigorous analysis, thematic funds can offer *targeted expression of belief*. For instance, if an investor understands the policy tailwinds behind infrastructure development, and can evaluate the cyclical nature of capital goods, they might allocate a portion of their equity exposure to an infrastructure fund—*not in lieu of diversification*, but as a complementary satellite holding. Likewise, ESG funds might appeal to investors with ethical mandates or environmental considerations, offering alignment between capital and conscience. But even in such cases, exposure should be proportionate to the investor's overall strategy and tolerance for volatility.

From a risk management perspective, there is wisdom in limiting thematic or sectoral fund allocation to a small percentage of one's total portfolio—often no more than 5–10% for most retail investors. This allows for potential upside participation without threatening portfolio stability. It also imposes a discipline of prioritising core over conviction: keeping the majority of one's assets in diversified, broad-market instruments that do not hinge on any one narrative, no matter how compelling. As many seasoned investors will attest, the best long-term returns often come not from chasing breakthroughs but from *enduring exposure to boring, diversified assets.*

Another important factor to consider is fund manager discretion. Unlike index-based sector funds, many thematic funds are actively managed, meaning the fund manager has significant leeway in choosing how to express the theme. This introduces two layers of subjectivity: first, in defining what constitutes the theme (e.g. does a "technology fund" include fintech, cloud computing, semiconductors, or all of them?); and second, in selecting specific stocks. The risk here is that investor assumptions about the theme may not match the fund's actual holdings. This again underlines the importance of *reading the fund factsheet*, understanding portfolio composition, and not relying on fund titles or marketing narratives alone.

Furthermore, investors must distinguish between *strategic alignment* and *speculative concentration.* Strategic alignment is when a thematic fund fits into an overarching asset allocation plan and is backed by clear reasoning and long-term conviction. Speculative concentration, on the other hand, occurs when the fund is bought impulsively—often after a period of strong performance—with little consideration for sector risk, valuation, or cyclical behaviour. The former approach can add texture and targeted returns to a mature portfolio. The latter often ends in disappointment and disillusionment.

A practical illustration comes from the performance of technology-themed mutual funds in the United States over the past decade. In the immediate aftermath of the 2008 financial crisis, those who invested early in tech funds—backed by genuine belief in cloud, mobile, and data-driven transformation—were well rewarded. But those who entered in late 2020, spurred by pandemic-fuelled rallies and high-profile IPOs, faced significant drawdowns as valuations corrected in 2022. The difference was not the underlying theme—it remained robust—but *the entry point, allocation size, and investor expectation.* This is where thematic investing becomes not just a financial, but a *psychological discipline.*

Ultimately, thematic and sectoral funds magnify everything—potential returns, potential losses, and emotional responses to both. They invite deeper participation in ideas investors care about, but demand a higher standard of self-awareness, analytical rigour, and portfolio discipline. They are not tools for beginners, nor for those looking for passive growth. But for the informed, cautious, and conviction-led investor, they offer a way to engage with markets not merely as abstract economic machines, but as *expressions of belief about the future.*

The challenge is to ensure that this belief is supported by evidence, integrated within broader strategy, and resilient against the inevitable cycles of hype and disillusionment. Because when focus becomes tunnel vision, the line between investing and gambling blurs. And no narrative—no matter how persuasive—should ever replace sound structure, adequate diversification, and a clear-eyed understanding of risk.

Chapter 4
The Wisdom of the Index

The world of investing, in all its complexity and apparent glamour, often seems to reward confidence more readily than competence. From the glass towers of London's financial districts to the modest home offices of retail traders, a common assumption prevails: those who bet boldly and intelligently must naturally achieve superior results. Yet beneath the surface—beyond stock-picking, hedge funds, and exclusive financial products—a quiet but profound shift has taken root. This shift does not hinge on prediction, but on replication. It does not chase outperformance, but embraces acceptance. Its instrument is the index fund.

To appreciate index investing, we must first confront a deceptively simple question: what does it mean to track an index? For many, the term evokes passivity or generic returns. But, in reality, an index fund exemplifies disciplined neutrality. It does not attempt to outsmart the market, forecast cycles, or uncover hidden winners. Instead, it mirrors a benchmark—be it the Nifty 50, S&P 500, or FTSE All-World—holding the same stocks in the same proportions. Think of it as following a carefully tested recipe rather than improvising with unfamiliar ingredients. There is no flourish, no heroics—and paradoxically, that absence of ego becomes its greatest asset.

The strength of this approach is evident when comparing index funds with actively managed alternatives. Research from Morningstar, S&P Dow Jones, and the Financial Times consistently demonstrates that most active fund managers fail to outperform their benchmark over long periods. This is no recent anomaly; it is a structural feature of modern markets. After fees, taxes, and transaction costs are accounted for, even the most adept managers struggle to maintain an edge. SPIVA reports reveal that over 80% of active equity funds lag their indices over 15-year spans. The market, in truth, is often smarter than the majority of its participants.

Yet such a reality challenges intuition. It confronts the human need for control. Investors wish to pick the "right" fund, anticipate the next Amazon, sidestep crises. Fund houses willingly nurture that desire, often levying high fees for what amounts to guesswork wrapped in spreadsheets. Index funds, in contrast, quietly reject the cult of expertise. They suggest: you do not need to outthink the market—only to trust it. This is not resignation; it is an empirically grounded optimism.

Index investing, therefore, is more than a tactic—it is a philosophy. It embodies faith in capitalism's resilience, the compounding of innovation, and the long-term growth of publicly listed enterprises. Choosing a broad-market index signals a belief that companies will adapt, evolve, and create value—not without setbacks or turbulence, but consistently enough to reward patience. Ironically, by resisting the urge to chase the extraordinary, index investors often achieve superior results over time.

Yet simplicity should not be confused with triviality. Not all index funds are identical. Tracking errors, hidden costs, and the breadth of the index can dramatically influence outcomes. A fund following a narrow index like the Nifty 50 behaves differently from one tracking a global universe like the MSCI World Index. Selection is not merely about minimising expense ratios—it demands alignment with one's financial goals, risk appetite, and investment horizon.

For newcomers, the appeal of index funds lies in their simplicity—but this simplicity is conditional on informed choices. Does the fund replicate the index accurately, or use selective sampling? Are dividends reinvested or distributed? Is the managing house disciplined and transparent? These questions require neither a finance degree nor complex calculations, but a willingness to engage thoughtfully rather than oversimplify.

Emotional resilience is another virtue of index investing. It frees investors from the need for constant monitoring, sector rotation, or market timing. For professionals pressed for time, parents juggling responsibilities, or students beginning their financial journeys, index funds offer participation in long-term wealth creation without intellectual exhaustion. Returns in any single year may not be extraordinary—but over decades, the compounding of steady, average returns can be remarkable.

Consider a historical example. An investor placing £10,000 into an S&P 500 index fund in 1990, leaving it untouched, would see it grow to over £200,000 by 2020, despite recessions, political upheavals, and global crises. Active funds appeared and faded, stars rose and fell, predictions faltered. The index endured—not through brilliance, but through systematic consistency. Its power lies in removing emotion, friction, and hubris from the equation.

Critiques exist. Some argue that widespread indexing may impair price discovery; others worry about passive funds' influence on corporate governance. These concerns are legitimate. Yet for individual investors lacking institutional advantages, the practical benefits of index funds far outweigh theoretical risks. No strategy is flawless, but some are robust. Indexing belongs to that category.

This chapter will unravel the mystique surrounding index funds: how they function, what they track, and why they matter. It will show you how to read fund factsheets, discern genuine simplicity from superficial appearances, and select index funds with clarity. More importantly, it will reveal the psychological liberation that comes from relinquishing the drive to beat the market—and instead, aligning with it.

Sometimes, the wisest move is not striving harder, but stepping back, thinking clearly, and embracing a strategy that wins quietly over time.

What Index Funds Actually Track:

Ask a typical investor what an index fund is, and you'll likely hear vague references to "the market," "passive investing," or perhaps "something low-cost." Press further, and many will admit they don't actually know what an index fund *tracks*, or even what an index *is*. This gap in understanding is not merely semantic—it reflects a deeper misconception about what investors are really buying into when they choose an index fund over an actively managed one. The truth is this: an index fund is not a vague bet on stability or a shortcut for the uninformed. It is a rigorously structured vehicle designed to *mirror the collective performance of a clearly defined segment of the financial world.*

And it does so by following a blueprint—an index—with far more discipline than many human investors are capable of.

At its essence, an index is a curated list. It represents a specific slice of the market—a set of companies selected according to predefined rules. The FTSE 100, for instance, includes the 100 largest companies listed on the London Stock Exchange by market capitalisation. The S&P 500 comprises 500 large-cap U.S. stocks, weighted by size and sector. The Nifty 50 covers the top Indian equities. These indices are not arbitrarily assembled. Each one reflects an agreed-upon methodology that determines which companies are included, in what proportion, and when changes are made. This rules-based structure allows an index fund to replicate the composition of the index with mathematical precision—not because it is smart, but because it is *systematic.*

Think of it this way: investing in an index fund is like following a meticulously tested recipe. You don't improvise. You measure ingredients exactly. You trust the process, not the performance of your palate. Active investing, by contrast, is akin to cooking without a recipe—selecting ingredients based on hunches, tastes, or the latest food trend. Sometimes you end up with a culinary masterpiece. More often, the dish is mediocre—and you don't know why. Index funds remove the guesswork. They eliminate human discretion in favour of repeatable logic. That logic is the index.

This distinction is crucial because it reframes what the investor is actually doing. When you buy into an index fund, you are *not* betting on a particular fund manager's insight, timing, or temperament. You are buying exposure to the collective outcome of a defined market segment. Whether that's the top 500 U.S. companies, global emerging markets, or a basket of government bonds, your returns will reflect the average performance of that group—*minus a very small fee.* You aren't trying to outperform the market. You *are* the market, in proportion to the slice you've chosen.

Why does this matter? Because index funds are often dismissed as "uninspired" or "lazy" investing. In reality, they are *some of the most transparent, disciplined, and intellectually honest financial products available.* Every aspect of an index fund can be explained: which securities it holds, why it holds them, how often it rebalances, and what it costs. There are no black-box algorithms, no secret sauce, no personality cults surrounding a star fund manager. What you see is precisely what you get.

This transparency makes index funds uniquely suited for investors who value clarity over charisma. For instance, consider an investor seeking broad exposure to global equities. They could choose a fund that tracks the MSCI All Country World Index—a benchmark representing over 2,900 companies from 23 developed and 27 emerging markets. By investing in a fund that mimics this index, they instantly gain proportional exposure to the global economy, without needing to evaluate thousands of individual stocks, industries, or countries. The index has already done the curating. The fund simply follows that map.

And yet, not all maps are equal. Some indices are broader, more representative, or better constructed than others. Some are tilted toward particular sectors, regions, or weighting methods. For example, the Nasdaq-100 is heavily skewed towards technology companies, which means an index fund tracking it will behave very differently from one tracking the broader S&P 500. This is where intelligent index investing begins—not with blindly trusting "passive" products, but with understanding what the index actually represents. *Choosing an index fund is ultimately an exercise in selecting the right blueprint for your financial goals.*

It's also important to dispel the myth that indices never change. While their rules are fixed, their constituents are not. Companies that no longer meet the criteria—due to declining market capitalisation, poor performance, or delisting—are removed, and others are added. This natural churn ensures that the index remains aligned with its original purpose. In effect, index funds *dynamically evolve* without requiring the investor to lift a finger. It is a form of passive agility—precise, automatic, and devoid of emotional interference.

Some critics argue that index funds simply ride on the coattails of active investors who do the hard work of price discovery. This view assumes a zero-sum game, where passive investors are parasites in the ecosystem. But this critique misunderstands the scale of the modern market. The majority of equity assets may now be indexed in some regions, but liquidity, volatility, and pricing continue to be driven by active participants. More importantly, from the perspective of an individual investor, the question is not whether indexing is theoretically elegant—it is whether it *delivers dependable, low-cost exposure to market returns over time.* The data is unequivocal: it does.

Moreover, index funds introduce an overlooked psychological benefit—*they reduce the temptation to intervene.* Active funds require ongoing decisions: Should I switch funds? Is this manager still outperforming? Should I reallocate based on economic news? Index funds, by contrast, *free the investor from performance anxiety.* There is no "beating" to monitor, no strategy to second-guess. You are not trying to win a game. You are content to own a stake in the game itself.

And that brings us to a philosophical dimension often absent in technical discussions. Index investing represents a humble stance in an industry dominated by bravado. It acknowledges that no one can consistently predict the best-performing stocks or sectors. It prefers diversification to concentration, evidence over excitement, and discipline over drama. For many, this humility feels countercultural. But it is precisely what makes indexing such a powerful wealth-building tool—*especially for those who want their money to grow quietly, predictably, and with minimal interference.*

At its best, then, an index fund is not a compromise. It is a deliberate strategy rooted in financial science and behavioural realism. It offers clarity where active management offers opacity. It demands almost nothing of the investor while delivering almost everything required for long-term success: diversification, cost efficiency, transparency, and alignment with market growth. The only requirement is the willingness to understand what you're tracking—and why.

In the pages that follow, we will explore not just how index funds operate, but how to select among them wisely. From understanding tracking error and replication methods to distinguishing between cap-weighted and equal-weighted indices, this subchapter will equip you with the insight to treat index investing not as a generic shortcut, but as a precision tool. Because *when you know exactly what you're tracking, you're no longer investing passively—you're investing with purpose.*

Why Most Professionals Can't Beat the Index:

It is one of the most quietly inconvenient truths in the world of investing: most professionals—the people paid handsomely to analyse markets, research companies, time entries and exits, and construct portfolios—*consistently fail to outperform* the humble index fund. The data is not ambiguous. It is not new. And it is not disputed by serious scholars. Yet the investment industry, propelled by confidence and cloaked in complexity, continues to market active management as a premium service worthy of premium fees. This disconnect between performance and perception lies at the heart of a cognitive dissonance—where ego, illusion, and economics converge.

The scale of this underperformance is staggering. In its ongoing SPIVA (S&P Indices Versus Active) scorecards, S&P Dow Jones Indices tracks the results of active fund managers globally. Their findings are both robust and relentless. In the United States, for example, over a 10-year horizon, more than 85% of actively managed large-cap funds underperform their benchmark index. Extend the time horizon to 20 years, and that figure climbs past 90%. These are not cherry-picked datasets. They span thousands of funds, account for survivorship bias (where poorly performing funds are shut down and quietly forgotten), and are consistent across geographies. In Europe, India, Canada, and Australia, the story is largely the same. Time is the great revealer—and time, almost always, sides with the index.

This empirical reality is deeply uncomfortable for the financial services industry. After all, it undercuts the central promise sold to clients: that expert insight, proprietary research, and tactical management can deliver superior returns. The active manager's pitch rests on differentiation. But the results suggest commoditisation. If a low-cost index fund can achieve the same or better outcomes with far greater reliability, the rationale for paying higher fees begins to dissolve.

Why, then, do most professionals underperform? The answer is not incompetence. It is structural. Active managers face a range of headwinds that collectively sabotage their attempts to beat the market. First and foremost is *cost.* An index fund typically charges 0.05% to 0.25% annually in fees. Active funds often charge 1% to 2% or more. That difference may seem minor, but over time, the compounding effect of higher costs is brutal. Imagine two portfolios earning 7% gross annually—one paying 0.1% in fees, the other 1.5%. Over 30 years, the low-cost option will yield nearly 25% more in cumulative returns. *This fee drag alone is sufficient to explain much of the active manager underperformance.*

Next is *the difficulty of repeated outperformance.* The market is a dynamic, highly competitive arena. Every advantage is fleeting. Information that once provided an edge is quickly arbitraged away. Even talented managers struggle to maintain their edge as assets under management grow. Large funds face liquidity constraints—they cannot easily shift in and out of positions without impacting prices. This means that even when they identify attractive opportunities, they may not be able to exploit them fully. Moreover, the statistical likelihood of sustained outperformance is tiny. According to research by Vanguard and Morningstar, very few managers who outperform over one five-year period are able to do so again in the next. *Skill may exist, but it is exceedingly rare and nearly impossible to identify in advance.*

The behavioural dynamics of fund management further compound the problem. Fund managers are not just navigating markets; they are navigating *clients.* They operate under pressure from investors, boards, marketing teams, and compliance officers. This introduces short-termism. Managers often tilt portfolios not toward optimal long-term outcomes, but toward what looks justifiable in quarterly reviews. Risk-averse decisions, style drift, or closet indexing—where active funds begin to mirror the index to avoid embarrassment—are all rational responses to institutional pressures. But they erode the core value proposition of active management.

Paradoxically, the higher the fee, the more likely a fund is to *underperform.* This is counterintuitive to most consumers. In nearly every other industry—hotels, restaurants, electronics—higher price implies higher quality. But in investing, cost and value often move in *opposite* directions. Nobel Laureate William Sharpe put this succinctly in his famous paper, *The Arithmetic of Active Management* (1991). He demonstrated that, before fees, the average active dollar must earn the same return as the average passive dollar—because both groups own the same market. After fees, however, the active dollar *must* underperform. It is not conjecture. It is *mathematical certainty.*

This realisation led other Nobel-winning economists—like Eugene Fama and Kenneth French—to reinforce the academic case for passive investing. Their research on the Efficient Market Hypothesis and factor-based returns showed that markets, while not perfectly efficient, are efficient *enough* that most efforts to beat them are wasted energy. Active management, they argue, becomes less about skill and more about luck—a roulette game played with expensive chips.

Even when a successful active manager emerges, identifying them in advance is close to impossible. Hindsight bias tempts us to believe we could have spotted the stars early—Peter Lynch, Joel Greenblatt, or Terry Smith. But most of these names gained fame only after decades of performance. For every visible winner, there are dozens of forgotten failures. This is known as the *survivor bias* problem—our attention is naturally drawn to success stories, obscuring the larger field of mediocrity.

And yet, the myth persists. Investors continue to chase outperforming funds, often buying in just as the manager's hot streak fades. Morningstar once produced a study showing that investor *returns* (dollar-weighted) often lagged fund *returns* (time-weighted), simply because people tend to enter and exit funds at precisely the wrong times. Chasing performance leads to overpaying for past success and abandoning strategy during short-term dips. Index funds, by contrast, remove this temptation. *They are built for consistency, not charisma.*

This doesn't mean all active management is worthless. There are niche markets—such as small-cap stocks, emerging markets, or distressed debt—where information asymmetries still exist. In such pockets, skilful managers may generate alpha. But even here, the odds are long, and due diligence is crucial. The question intelligent investors must ask is not whether outperformance is *theoretically possible*, but whether it is *likely, persistent, and accessible to them*. For most, the answer is no.

What makes index investing so quietly revolutionary is not its lack of ambition, but its rejection of hubris. It says: "I do not need to predict winners. I do not believe in market timing. I trust in broad participation and low friction." It is a philosophy rooted in humility and rationalism—qualities not often celebrated in financial marketing, but profoundly effective over decades. By owning the market, index investors accept market returns as *sufficient*. And in doing so, they avoid the punishing costs of trying to do better.

There is also a moral dimension to this argument. When advisors sell high-fee, actively managed products to retail clients—despite knowing the overwhelming odds against their success—they are not merely mispricing products; they are misplacing trust. Transparency, accountability, and fiduciary duty demand a higher standard. Recommending index funds is not about surrender. It is about respecting evidence, minimising harm, and aligning incentives between advisor and client.

The arc of investing history is bending toward simplicity. Institutional giants like Norway's sovereign wealth fund, Warren Buffett's estate instructions, and the default settings of modern retirement plans all point to indexing. This is not ideological rigidity. It is a reflection of data, experience, and risk awareness. As investors mature in their thinking, many come to realise that beating the market is not only unlikely—it may not even be necessary. *Capturing the market is already enough to build extraordinary wealth—without the stress, fees, or fragility of chasing stars.*

In the pages that follow, we'll explore the deeper implications of this quiet revolution. We'll see how index funds don't merely offer efficiency; they restore trust. They shift the narrative from prediction to participation. And they ask us to consider a subtle but transformative idea: that perhaps the wisest strategy is not to outsmart the system, but to stop trying.

Indexing as an Act of Trust:

At first glance, index investing may appear mechanical—a dry exercise in replication, statistics, and cost efficiency. But beneath the spreadsheets and low-fee wrappers lies something more profound. To invest in an index is to cast a long-term vote of confidence—not just in the arithmetic of markets, but in the resilience of capitalism itself. Index investing, properly understood, is not a retreat from belief; it is its most rational expression. It assumes that despite periodic volatility, political upheaval, or economic contractions, the sum of human enterprise will rise. And that belief, executed with calm and clarity, is what ultimately compounds.

This is not sentimentality masquerading as strategy. The most disciplined investors in the world—sovereign wealth funds, endowments, and retirement systems—have been shifting aggressively into index-based allocations over the past two decades. Why? Not because they have given up hope of outperformance, but because they've come to understand that *markets work*. Imperfectly, inefficiently at times, but directionally—with force. The aggregate output of businesses around the world—across borders, sectors, and decades—is a remarkable engine. By indexing, you attach yourself to that engine without the distraction of trying to steer it.

To index is to accept that no one can consistently forecast the next breakthrough technology, the next market downturn, or the next political surprise. It is to relinquish the illusion of perfect foresight and replace it with broad participation. This, paradoxically, is what gives index investing its moral power. *It's an act of humility wrapped in discipline.*

Capitalism, though flawed, is a system built on adaptation. Markets are not static entities; they evolve, absorb shocks, correct mistakes, and reallocate resources in response to incentives. An index fund is not a passive lump of stocks—it is a living reflection of the economy's capacity to evolve. When certain sectors underperform, others rise. When companies fail, they fall out of the index, replaced by more efficient competitors. This constant rebalancing is built into the DNA of the index. You don't need to predict which companies will dominate tomorrow—you only need to believe that, in aggregate, the system is self-improving.

That belief is not naïve. It is informed by history. Consider the past century. The Great Depression. World War II. The stagflation of the 1970s. The dot-com bust. The global financial crisis. A pandemic. In every instance, equity markets recovered—not because of blind optimism, but because capital was continuously reallocated to more productive uses. If you had invested in a global equity index at almost any point in modern history and held it for 20 years, you would have come out ahead—often significantly so. *This is the quiet power of resilience expressed through ownership.*

Index investing stands in contrast to the culture of prediction that dominates financial commentary. The financial media thrives on noise—quarterly earnings surprises, economic forecasts, and the cult of personality around fund managers. But none of this noise has been shown to produce better outcomes for long-term investors. Indexing steps outside that carnival. It doesn't pretend to know what comes next. It bets that *something* will come next, and that participating in the broad story of progress is reward enough.

There is also a deeply egalitarian quality to index investing. Historically, access to markets was stratified—reserved for the wealthy, the advised, or the institutionally connected. The advent of index funds democratised access. For a few pounds or dollars, anyone can now own a diversified stake in thousands of companies. No insider tips required. No PhDs in economics. No trading screens. Just patient capital and a low-cost vehicle. This shift—quiet and profound—has arguably done more for financial inclusion than decades of regulatory reform.

And yet, index investing is often derided by its critics as "settling for average." This criticism misunderstands both the goal and the mechanics. Indexing does not aim for mediocrity; it aims for *efficiency*. It does not try to outguess the market because it recognises the futility of the chase. The "average" return of the market, compounded consistently and cheaply over time, has historically outperformed the vast majority of high-fee, high-risk alternatives. *To accept the market is not to settle; it is to align.*

This alignment is strategic, but also psychological. Investors often fall prey to behaviours that undermine their returns: chasing performance, timing the market, reacting emotionally to volatility. Index funds create distance from these tendencies. They replace the drama of "what should I buy next?" with the calm of "am I saving consistently?" They reframe investing as a system, not a series of bets. In doing so, they allow ordinary people to build wealth without becoming investment obsessives.

This is a form of self-trust, too. Indexing asks us to decouple success from brilliance. You don't need to be the smartest person in the room. You don't need the perfect timing or the next big idea. You need time, conviction, and the ability to stay out of your own way. It is a mindset shift as much as a strategy: *less control, more consistency.*

But indexing is also, at its heart, a collective bet on the future. Every time you allocate capital to a broad-based index, you are saying: I believe that people will continue to create value. That businesses will adapt. That innovation will rise. That the world, in net terms, will be worth more tomorrow than it is today. This belief does not require blind faith. It rests on incentives, systems, and the observable outcomes of decades. Still, it is a belief. And investing without belief—investing purely for return, detached from a view of progress—is ultimately fragile. It collapses under stress, because there is no foundational "why."

Consider the structure of an index itself. It is inherently self-cleansing. The worst-performing companies are gradually diminished in influence, while the most successful become dominant. A fund tracking the S&P 500 in 2000 held large positions in companies like General Electric, ExxonMobil, and Citigroup. Today, it holds Apple, Microsoft, and Nvidia. No committee needed. No heroic analyst calls. Just a system designed to evolve with the world it measures. *This built-in adaptability is one of indexing's most underrated strengths.*

There are, of course, thoughtful critiques of index investing. Some worry about concentration risk, especially in market-cap-weighted indices. Others raise concerns about corporate governance and the role of passive investors in holding companies accountable. These are valid points and worth engaging. But they are not arguments against indexing per se—they are arguments for evolving how we *implement* indexing. Smart investors should stay informed about how their funds operate, vote proxies, and align their choices with their values. Index investing is not a blank cheque. It is an intelligent default.

For all its mathematical neatness, indexing also carries ethical weight. It is a rejection of extractive finance—the part of the industry that enriches itself through churn, complexity, and opacity. It is a protest against promises of outperformance that rarely materialise. And it is an embrace of a quieter, more grounded relationship with money—one based not on conquest, but on coherence.

Ultimately, index investing is a modern expression of an ancient idea: that *patience pays*. That by aligning with the broader arc of human enterprise—and avoiding the seduction of shortcuts—we place ourselves in a position to benefit from what the world becomes. It is not a theory. It is not a trend. It is a philosophy backed by decades of empirical evidence and a worldview that remains, in the best sense, hopeful.

And that hope—rational, tested, and resilient—is what turns indexing from a technical decision into a transformative one. You are not just buying a fund. You are buying a belief: that progress, though uneven, is real. That capitalism, for all its flaws, has lifted billions. That innovation persists. That participation matters. And that staying invested—calmly, quietly, consistently—is not an act of resignation, but one of trust.

Choosing the Right Index Fund:

The genius of index investing lies in its simplicity—but that simplicity is often misunderstood. Many assume that all index funds are functionally identical, like photocopies of the same idea. They are not. Beneath the placid surface of the term "index fund" lies a complex and consequential set of differences. Choosing the wrong one can quietly erode decades of compounding. Choosing the right one, on the other hand, can provide unmatched efficiency, reliability, and peace of mind. The stakes are higher than they appear.

At the heart of index investing is replication: the goal is to mirror the performance of a benchmark index as closely as possible. But indexes come in many shapes and sizes—from broad market trackers like the FTSE All-World or S&P 500, to narrower instruments focused on emerging markets, specific sectors, or dividend-paying stocks. The fund's objective is not just to follow that index—it must do so *with precision and discipline.* Herein lies the first critical differentiator: *tracking error*. This is the degree to which a fund deviates from the performance of its benchmark. A good index fund should hug its index closely. Even small, persistent deviations can compound into meaningful shortfalls over time.

Tracking error is influenced by multiple variables—portfolio management technique, cash drag, transaction timing, and sampling methodology. Some funds attempt full replication, owning every security in the index in exact proportion. Others use optimisation or stratified sampling, particularly when tracking very large or illiquid indices. These methods are not inherently flawed, but they introduce variability. When selecting a fund, a consistently low tracking error is not a marketing footnote—it is a measure of craft.

Equally essential is cost. Index investing is built on the premise that lower fees translate into higher net returns. Yet "low cost" is relative. A fund with a 0.10% expense ratio may seem cheap, but if there is a near-identical fund charging 0.04%, the difference—though seemingly trivial—adds up over a 30-year horizon. Compounding doesn't care how small a percentage looks today. It amplifies every basis point. And while active funds often charge well over 1% per annum, index funds still vary widely depending on the provider, the domicile, the platform, and the share class. It is not unusual to see identical strategies priced very differently across geographies.

Cost, however, is not only about the expense ratio. Investors must also evaluate *hidden friction points*: bid-ask spreads for ETFs, minimum investment requirements, tax efficiency, and trading costs on platforms. These variables may not appear in glossy fund brochures, but they matter. In particular, funds domiciled in tax-efficient jurisdictions, or those structured as accumulating share classes, may provide better after-tax outcomes for certain investors. The cost of ownership is more than the headline figure.

Scope is the third crucial axis. Not all indices are created equal. Some are broad and inclusive, offering global diversification. Others are more concentrated or rules-based. For example, a market-cap-weighted index will tilt toward the largest companies by design, while an equal-weighted index will favour smaller, more volatile constituents. Some funds track "smart beta" indices—blends of value, momentum, or volatility screens. These may promise superior outcomes but often blur the line between passive indexing and active filtering. *Investors must be clear whether they are buying exposure to the market or a thesis about it.*

Scope also determines exposure gaps. A fund tracking the S&P 500 gives you a slice of the largest US companies—but nothing beyond that. An FTSE All-World fund, by contrast, gives exposure to developed and emerging markets alike. The choice isn't trivial. It reflects a view about global capital, diversification, and long-term opportunity. It also shapes currency risk, political exposure, and sector balance. The right fund, therefore, depends not only on what you want to own—but what you want to *avoid* owning too narrowly.

There is also the question of governance. Behind every index fund is a fund house: Vanguard, BlackRock, Fidelity, State Street, and others. Each has its own incentives, stewardship philosophy, and business model. Some are mutually owned. Others are for-profit conglomerates. When you invest in an index fund, you are not just buying a basket of stocks—you are entering into a long-term relationship with the entity that manages it. Do they vote proxies in line with your values? Do they lend securities responsibly? Do they disclose practices transparently? These questions often go unasked, but they should not. *Low cost should never mean low scrutiny.*

Reputation alone is insufficient. Some providers use marketing muscle to create a halo of trustworthiness while layering funds with operational complexity. There are index funds with front-end sales loads, 12b-1 distribution fees, and kickbacks to intermediaries—all dressed up in low-fee language. The discipline of indexing only works if it is executed without conflicts. A fund that charges 1% to track a basic index is functionally abusive, no matter how slick the branding. *Transparency is a litmus test for integrity.*

Even among legitimate providers, subtle design decisions matter. Consider fund rebalancing frequency. Index constituents change periodically, and how a fund implements those changes—whether it tracks reconstitutions daily, monthly, or quarterly—affects performance and tax efficiency. Timing mismatches can generate slippage or unnecessary capital gains. Good funds manage these transitions smoothly. Lesser funds don't.

Another overlooked factor is currency exposure. A UK investor buying a US index fund is implicitly taking a view on the sterling-dollar exchange rate, whether they mean to or not. Some funds offer hedged share classes to mitigate this risk. Others do not. Currency swings can be significant over time—and while they may wash out over decades, short-term volatility can affect investor behaviour. Understanding what you're exposed to—and what you're not—is part of choosing wisely.

There is no perfect fund. But there are funds that are *fit for purpose.* To identify them, thoughtful investors must go beyond brand and brochure. They must read the Key Investor Information Document (KIID), understand the index methodology, evaluate real costs, and inspect the fund's behaviour over time. Past performance is not the goal—but consistency in delivering what the fund *promises* is.

A useful framework for choosing the right index fund includes a handful of questions. What exactly does the fund track—and why was that index chosen? What is the fund's total expense ratio, and how does it compare to peers? How closely has it tracked its index historically? What is the replication method? How frequently is the index reconstituted? Who manages the fund, and what are their incentives? Are there tax considerations or platform-specific charges that affect net outcomes?

Too often, investors look at past returns and stop there. But the past is not repeatable. What is repeatable are *structures*: low costs, tight tracking, sound governance. The best index funds are boring by design. They do not outperform wildly, nor do they collapse in crisis. They deliver predictable exposure to a defined basket, year after year, with minimal friction. This predictability, paradoxically, is what makes them so powerful.

Choosing the right index fund is not about finding a hidden gem. It is about eliminating unnecessary noise and narrowing your focus to the factors that actually matter. This is where discipline meets judgement. It is not glamorous. But it is profoundly effective.

In the end, an index fund is a tool. Its usefulness depends on its construction, its clarity, and its cost. When chosen well, it becomes more than just a portfolio component—it becomes the backbone of a philosophy: that markets work, that simplicity scales, and that trust—earned through rigour—deserves your capital. The best funds don't just mirror markets. They reflect your commitment to investing with reason, not reaction. And that, over time, is what builds real wealth.

Chapter 5
Actively Managed Funds—When, Why, and If

For all the attention lavished on index funds and passive strategies, actively managed funds remain a significant—and often misunderstood—corner of the investment landscape. They are simultaneously lauded and dismissed, sometimes without a clear grasp of what they actually entail. Too often, conviction masquerades as comprehension. This chapter invites you to set aside assumptions, whether sceptical or enthusiastic, and approach active management with clarity, precision, and curiosity.

At its essence, active management is a framework for deliberate decision-making. A fund manager, or a team thereof, is charged with choosing what to buy, when to buy it, and when to sell. The objective is straightforward in theory: outperform a benchmark. It appeals naturally—why settle for average if better returns are attainable? Yet the reality is less forgiving. Most active funds, evaluated over meaningful time horizons and net of fees, fail to beat their benchmarks. This is not pessimism—it is an empirical fact.

That said, active management is far from worthless. Its value is conditional, much like the difference between general medicine and specialised surgery. Expertise can justify an active fund's existence, but it must be rare, deliberate, and commensurate with cost. More often than not, it is neither. Occasionally, it is.

To discern when active funds are warranted, one must strip away marketing gloss. Managers are neither magicians nor gamblers. At their best, they are disciplined analysts operating under structured frameworks. Their pursuit is mispricing—identifying instances where the market undervalues or overvalues assets, and attempting to monetise those anomalies before correction. It is a calculated gamble, not a roll of the dice, and it hinges on outseeing the collective intelligence of millions with access to the same data.

Managers deploy four primary tools in pursuit of alpha: security selection, sector rotation, market timing, and risk concentration. Each opens the door to potential outperformance while simultaneously increasing the likelihood of deviation from the benchmark. Deviations are not inherently negative. In periods of high dispersion—when sector or regional returns diverge sharply—skilled active managers can add measurable value. Similarly, in less liquid markets, such as small caps, emerging markets, or distressed debt, inefficiencies persist longer, providing opportunities for those with insight and discipline. Yet these scenarios are exceptions, not justifications for indiscriminate allocation.

The complexity of active funds extends beyond their mechanics; it lies in the behaviour they provoke. Research—from Morningstar to DALBAR—demonstrates that investors frequently underperform the funds they hold. They chase performance, buying after rallies and selling after drawdowns. This "behaviour gap" means that even well-managed funds may fail to deliver promised outcomes simply because human behaviour interferes.

Herein lies the paradox: active funds, designed for patience, conviction, and alignment with strategy, often attract the opposite. They become vehicles for short-term speculation, transforming disciplined portfolios into rolling performance scorecards. The costs—both explicit and opportunity-related—are substantial.

Evaluating an active fund requires a disciplined approach, anchored by four critical dimensions: cost, consistency, conviction, and context.

Cost is fundamental. Active funds charge more than passive alternatives. That is justified only if the service produces net value. Fees act as a structural hurdle: a fund charging 1.5% annually but underperforming its benchmark by 1% is mathematically self-defeating.

Consistency is next. A capable manager is an architect, not a magician. They must adhere to a documented framework and maintain repeatable discipline. Periodic underperformance is inevitable, especially in momentum-driven markets, but it is the coherence of strategy—rather than short-term results—that signals genuine skill.

Conviction is revealed through portfolio concentration and the willingness to diverge meaningfully from benchmarks. Many "active" funds are closet indexers, barely departing from index allocations while levying higher fees. These funds deliver neither protection nor potential.

Finally, context matters. An active fund cannot be assessed in isolation. It must be evaluated within the portfolio's broader architecture. Does it complement or double existing exposures? Does it introduce understood, acceptable risk? Is it purchased for narrative appeal or as part of a coherent thesis? These considerations are essential to intelligent selection.

The broader lesson is that active management is not obsolete; it is conditional. It rewards informed investors, penalises the impulsive, and demands purposeful engagement. When deployed strategically—where information asymmetry exists, when a fund demonstrates a clear edge, and when deviation from passive exposure is justified—it can succeed. The burden of proof, however, rests squarely with the fund. Performance must be demonstrable, philosophy transparent.

This chapter examines all these facets: the mechanisms active managers employ, distinguishing skill from luck, the conditions under which active funds justify their fees, and how investor behaviour can undermine even excellent strategy. The four-factor lens—cost, consistency, conviction, context—provides a rigorous framework for evaluation.

The objective is not to persuade for or against active funds. It is to equip you with the knowledge to decide for yourself, calmly and critically. Stripped of hype, hero narratives, and marketing, active management is not mystical. It is structured, demanding scrutiny, rewarding rigour, and, when approached judiciously, capable of earning its keep.

What Active Management Actually Does:

At a glance, the term "active management" sounds deceptively vague—perhaps even promotional. Fund advertisements often romanticise it with glossy phrases like "hands-on expertise" or "dynamic strategy." But these marketing euphemisms rarely explain the essence of what an active fund manager actually *does*. To understand active management properly, one must strip away the industry's abstraction and observe the mechanics underneath with clinical precision. What emerges is neither mysticism nor miracle—it's a structure of decisions built around conviction, constraints, and calculated bets.

An active fund manager's job is simple to define but difficult to do well: they aim to deliver returns above a specified benchmark. This excess return—referred to in financial literature as *alpha*—is the holy grail of active investing. The benchmark could be a broad market index like the FTSE 100, the S&P 500, or a sector-specific composite. Regardless of which, the active manager is not trying to match it—they are trying to beat it. And every decision they make is a vote for or against consensus.

At the core of this decision-making structure lie three principal levers: security selection, asset allocation, and timing. *Security selection* involves choosing specific stocks, bonds, or other instruments that the manager believes are mispriced. This requires detailed research into balance sheets, industry trends, macroeconomic indicators, competitive dynamics, and valuation metrics. A manager might look at a company's cash flow projections, interview management, run discounted cash flow models, and build scenarios under different economic conditions. These aren't hunches—they're hypotheses backed by models. But they are still bets.

The second lever—*asset allocation*—involves deciding how much capital to assign to various asset classes or sectors. For instance, should a global equity fund have 40% exposure to North America and 20% to emerging Asia? Should it lean into consumer staples or financials? Should it raise cash in times of volatility or stay fully invested? Each of these questions leads to a strategic posture, and that posture shapes the risk-return profile of the fund. Allocation isn't a passive consequence—it's a series of assumptions made visible.

Timing, the third lever, is perhaps the most contentious. Good active managers don't try to predict short-term price movements—they try to assess where value is misaligned relative to price. But their decisions still have a temporal component. If they believe a recession is imminent, they may rotate into defensive sectors; if they see a technological inflection point, they might overweight growth-oriented equities. These timing decisions are rarely binary—they unfold through marginal adjustments. But the cumulative impact of those adjustments can be significant.

It is crucial to understand that active management is not defined by activity alone. There are managers who trade often but think shallowly. There are others who trade rarely but with deep conviction. True active management is not measured by turnover—it is measured by *deviation*. That deviation, often quantified as *active share*, reflects how different the fund's holdings are from the benchmark. A high active share means the manager is genuinely making unique choices. A low active share suggests the fund is hugging the index while charging active fees—a phenomenon known as *closet indexing*. This is one of the most pernicious practices in asset management because it combines the cost of active with the substance of passive.

Distinguishing between skill and luck in active management is harder than it sounds. One year of outperformance proves nothing. Even five years may not suffice if the outperformance was driven by a single thematic tailwind. Investors must ask: *Was this performance the result of repeatable decisions or idiosyncratic windfall?* Academic work—particularly from Nobel laureates like Eugene Fama and Kenneth French—suggests that much of what appears to be skill is actually noise. Their research on efficient markets posits that prices already reflect all available information, making consistent outperformance statistically improbable.

Yet this view is not universally accepted. The counterpoint, articulated by practitioners and scholars like Michael Mauboussin, is that *markets may be efficient on average, but not always at the margins*. In less-covered segments—small-cap stocks, emerging markets, distressed debt—informational inefficiencies persist. In these pockets, skilled active managers can exploit temporary mispricings, and their edge stems from superior research, behavioural discipline, and long-term orientation. But even here, the hurdle is high. To justify higher fees, an active manager must deliver not just gross outperformance, but *net* outperformance after costs, taxes, and frictions.

An essential, though rarely acknowledged, dimension of active management is behavioural. Fund managers are not machines. They are subject to institutional pressures, career risk, peer comparisons, and client expectations. These forces can distort their decisions. For example, a manager may overweight popular stocks near quarter-end to improve their reportable performance (a practice dubbed "window dressing"), or they may avoid contrarian trades for fear of being too early. True conviction, then, is not just about insight—it is about the *willingness to act on that insight despite pressure.*

There is also an often-overlooked difference between *philosophical* and *tactical* active managers. Philosophical managers follow a disciplined investment framework—value, growth, quality, momentum—and adapt their strategy within it. Tactical managers, by contrast, tend to shift their approach opportunistically based on current conditions. Both can succeed, but the latter is more susceptible to narrative risk and short-termism. Investors must understand which type they are investing in, as the expectations and risk profiles differ markedly.

Importantly, the structure of the fund itself matters. Is the manager working with a concentrated portfolio or a broadly diversified one? Do they have the autonomy to deviate from the benchmark, or are they constrained by institutional guidelines? Do they eat their own cooking—that is, invest a meaningful portion of their own wealth in the fund they manage? These structural elements reveal a great deal about alignment and incentives. A manager who is paid to outperform but penalised for underperformance may make risk-averse choices that reduce both downside *and* upside. This is rational behaviour—but it may not serve the investor's interests.

To properly evaluate an active fund, investors must therefore look beyond returns. They must interrogate *process*. What is the manager's investment philosophy? How do they generate ideas, vet them, size positions, and exit trades? What is their research pipeline, and how are decisions made—individually, or by committee? What have they done during market stress? Did they double down with discipline or flinch under pressure? The answers to these questions are rarely found in marketing materials—they are found in performance commentaries, fund reports, and direct manager interviews. Doing this work is not easy. But it is necessary.

Even with all these insights, one must remain humble. The vast majority of professional active managers—despite excellent education, access to data, and research teams—do not outperform over 10- or 15-year horizons. According to SPIVA (S&P Indices Versus Active) reports, more than 85% of large-cap active managers underperform their benchmarks over the long term. That number is not anecdotal—it is systemic. It reflects the zero-sum nature of markets: for every winner, there must be a loser. And once costs are accounted for, the arithmetic becomes unforgiving.

But this reality does not make active management futile. It makes it selective. It demands that investors abandon hope as a strategy and replace it with scrutiny. If you are going to pay for judgment, make sure judgment is being applied. If you are going to deviate from the index, make sure that deviation is backed by process, not personality. And if you are going to believe in a manager, make sure that belief is based on evidence, not charisma.

Active management, when done properly, is not about frequent trading or flashy narratives. It is about calculated deviation, risk-aware decision-making, and an unrelenting focus on long-term value. It is not the antithesis of indexing—it is the complement *when used judiciously*. The goal is not to displace passive investing, but to augment it *when the case is strong*. And that case must be made with rigour—not rhetoric.

In this light, the question is no longer whether active management works. It is *when*, *why*, and *for whom* it works. Understanding what fund managers actually do—beyond the headlines, beyond the hype—is the first step toward answering that with clarity and conviction. Because once you demystify the mechanics, the real work begins—not in chasing performance, but in evaluating purpose.

When Active Funds Might Be Worth It:

Most of the time, the cold, uncompromising numbers favour passive investing. The majority of actively managed funds fail to outperform their benchmark indices over long periods, and when they do, the outperformance is rarely consistent. But even in this seemingly stacked equation, there are critical exceptions—contexts where active management doesn't just survive scrutiny but earns its keep. These are not the mainstream scenarios. They are specialised, situational, and often fleeting. Yet they reveal an important truth: *in finance, nuance beats dogma.*

To dismiss all active funds outright is to ignore where human insight, pattern recognition, and adaptive judgement still matter—particularly in parts of the market where information is scarce, liquidity is thin, or dislocation creates genuine mispricing. In these arenas, the right manager with the right approach can deliver returns that are not only superior to the benchmark but also uncorrelated with it—a rare and valuable quality in portfolio design.

This is where we must begin: not with a defence of active funds, but with a filter—*when might they be worth it, and how can we tell?*

The first clear case where active funds may be justified is in inefficient markets. Unlike the large-cap universe, where data is abundant, prices are closely watched, and institutional money flows dominate, inefficient markets tend to be under-analysed and overlooked. These include small-cap equities, emerging market debt, frontier markets, and niche fixed-income instruments like municipal bonds or high-yield corporate paper. In these arenas, inefficiencies persist longer and pricing anomalies are harder to arbitrage away. A skilled active manager here is not simply guessing—*they're exploiting informational asymmetry.* Research from institutions like Morningstar and S&P Dow Jones Indices consistently show that while large-cap active managers underperform their benchmarks, those operating in small-cap or less liquid corners of the market have a statistically higher probability of success, particularly net of fees when holding periods are longer.

A second domain where active funds might warrant attention is in navigating regime shifts—macro environments where the assumptions baked into index construction fail to hold. Index funds, by design, look backwards: they reflect the current market structure based on capitalisation or predefined rules. They don't anticipate. During major dislocations—think the global financial crisis of 2008, the COVID-19 pandemic's early stages, or major commodity supercycles—active managers who were willing to deviate meaningfully from consensus sometimes preserved or even grew capital while passive investors rode the turbulence. *The key term here is discretion*, something index funds by definition lack. A manager who rotates sector exposure quickly during an energy shock, or avoids bloated tech valuations before a correction, may outperform simply because they are allowed to think.

That said, discretion is not a virtue on its own. The question becomes whether the manager's decisions are grounded in repeatable skill rather than luck. Here we enter the more complex terrain of behavioural finance. Most investors—professional or not—suffer from cognitive biases. They chase performance, overreact to recent trends, and underestimate tail risks. Good active managers often function as behavioural counterweights. Instead of following the herd, they allocate contrarian capital with discipline, and in doing so may outperform not because of stock-picking genius per se, but because they avoid the worst of human error.

This points us to a less discussed but highly relevant reason to consider an active fund: *its role as a behavioural crutch.* When an investor recognises their own limitations—the tendency to panic during volatility, to overtrade, to oscillate between greed and fear—outsourcing the tactical decision-making to a fund with a long-term mandate and risk controls can be a form of disciplined delegation. In this light, the cost of active management can be reframed not just as a fee for performance but as a fee for *behavioural governance.* It is the same logic that justifies paying a personal trainer not merely for their expertise but for the consistency they enforce.

However, this benefit assumes that the fund manager's behaviour is more rational, more grounded, and more aligned with investor interests than the investor's own impulses. And this is far from a given. Many actively managed funds themselves suffer from short-termism, closet indexing, or compensation structures that reward asset gathering over long-term stewardship. This brings us to the most essential criterion. *incentive alignment*. The handful of active funds that merit attention tend to be those where the managers invest meaningfully in their own funds, limit AUM to preserve agility, and operate with transparency rather than marketing flair. In other words, the rare cases when *manager and investor interests converge over time*.

There is also the matter of flexibility. Unlike index funds that must hold what the benchmark dictates—no matter how overpriced, bloated, or broken—active funds can exit a holding entirely, sit on cash, or hedge. This optionality, if used prudently, can preserve capital when passivity would absorb losses by design. But it is a double-edged sword: flexibility invites judgment, and with judgment comes risk. The question for the investor becomes: *is the manager's judgment demonstrably better than randomness?*

Academic research has attempted to quantify this. A particularly influential study by Cremers and Petajisto introduced the concept of "active share"—a measure of how different a fund's holdings are from its benchmark. They found that funds with high active share and low turnover—indicating conviction and patience—tend to outperform over time, particularly after fees. But such funds are rare. Most active funds charge like mavericks and behave like benchmarks. It's the divergence between pricing and strategy that often dooms the category.

So what does this mean for a rational investor deciding between passive and active? The calculus isn't one-size-fits-all. If the goal is broad exposure to liquid, efficient markets like large-cap US equities, then index funds win on cost, transparency, and reliability. But if the investor has specific views about macroeconomic change, wants to access under-researched areas, or knows they're prone to self-defeating behaviours, then selective use of active funds—*emphasis on selective*—can add value.

A final consideration lies in time horizon. Many active strategies require a long gestation period to bear fruit. Investors who evaluate performance quarterly or even annually are likely to be disappointed or reactive. But those willing to commit capital for five to ten years, and to stick through underperformance if the thesis holds, are the ones most likely to benefit from the non-linear payoff of active conviction. *Patience, not just performance, determines whether the fee is justified.*

In the end, the role of active management in a portfolio should not be determined by marketing brochures or recent outperformance. It should be dictated by *strategy fit.* Does the fund operate in a domain where indexing is weak or blind? Does the manager demonstrate conviction, discipline, and skin in the game? Is the investor's behaviour improved by the fund's presence? These are the questions that matter—far more than past returns or star ratings.

The mistake is not in using active funds. The mistake is in using them blindly.

Performance Chasing: A Dangerous Addiction:

One of the most quietly destructive behaviours in personal investing is also among the most common: *chasing performance.* It is the tendency to shift money into funds that have recently outperformed and withdraw from those that have lagged—under the illusion that the past will project neatly into the future. This behaviour, repeated over time and across markets, is not a harmless quirk. It is a statistically proven drag on investor returns—*a behavioural tax that compounds invisibly.*

The data is unequivocal. Year after year, the average investor earns significantly less than the average fund. This isn't because fund managers are lying about performance or because markets are rigged. It's because investors themselves enter and exit at the wrong times—

buying high and selling low. Morningstar's "Investor Returns" studies have consistently shown this gap across asset classes and geographies. For example, while a mutual fund might generate an annualised 8% return over a decade, the average investor in that fund might only capture 5%—simply because they added money after rallies and pulled out during dips. The culprit isn't the fund. It's the timing. *And the timing is driven by emotion masked as strategy.*

The impulse to chase winners is deeply human. We're wired to seek patterns, reward certainty, and avoid discomfort. A fund with a one-year return of 25% looks like a safe bet. A fund down 10% feels toxic. But in investing, as in many domains, our instincts betray us. Short-term outperformance is often mean-reverting. That is, a fund that beats the market in one year tends to underperform in the next. This is not because the manager has suddenly become incompetent. It's because outperformance often stems from concentrated positions, market anomalies, or simple luck—none of which are reliably repeatable. *Reversion to the mean is not just a statistical tendency; it is the gravitational force of the markets.*

What makes performance chasing especially insidious is that it doesn't feel like speculation. It feels rational. A recent winner has momentum, visibility, endorsements. It appears in lists, newsletters, and comparison tables. Meanwhile, the underperforming fund looks inert. It inspires doubt. But this is where discipline must replace narrative. In most cases, a fund's recent underperformance is not a red flag—it's a natural outcome of its strategy, style, or exposure. Value funds lag growth during tech booms. International funds underperform when the dollar strengthens. Small caps fall out of favour during recessions. These cycles are not failures. They are expressions of risk premia playing out over time. *To abandon a long-term strategy mid-cycle is to miss the very returns it was designed to deliver.*

Consider a hypothetical investor who rotates annually into last year's top-performing equity fund. Over a decade, they will likely lag not only the market but also a simple buy-and-hold investor in an average-performing fund. This is not theory. Studies by firms like DALBAR and Vanguard confirm this with sobering clarity. DALBAR's long-term data shows that the average equity fund investor dramatically underperforms the market due to timing errors rooted in performance chasing. Vanguard's behavioural finance division found that staying invested consistently beats the vast majority of tactical reallocations, especially those based on short-term past returns.

The psychological mechanism is well-understood. After a period of market gains, optimism biases investors toward risk-taking. They reallocate into aggressive funds, overweight equities, or double down on sector winners. When the inevitable correction hits, fear sets in. The same investors then sell into weakness, rotate into perceived safe havens, or sit in cash "until things stabilise." The result? Selling low, buying high, and repeating the cycle. *This is not investing. It is emotional whiplash with a financial cost.*

But the problem isn't just individual psychology—it's institutional encouragement. Financial media, fund marketing, and even advisor incentives are often structured around short-term performance metrics. "Top 10 Funds of the Year" headlines, star ratings, and peer comparisons subtly nudge investors toward reactive decisions. Very few tools highlight long-term process discipline, downside protection, or the alignment of manager philosophy with investor objectives. In this noise-rich environment, performance becomes not just a metric—it becomes a marketing drug.

So how can investors break the cycle? It begins with a mindset shift: *stop thinking like a hunter, start thinking like a gardener.* Performance is not something to be captured in real time; it is something that grows through patience, consistency, and resilience. The goal is not to own the fund that just outperformed. It's to own the fund—or set of funds—that align with your goals, time horizon, and risk tolerance, and then to *stick with them through the uncomfortable middle.*

Discipline does not mean inaction. But it does mean structured action. Instead of reacting to last quarter's numbers, investors should assess whether their fund's strategy is intact. Has the manager deviated from the stated process? Have fees crept up unjustifiably? Is the fund still behaving in a way that matches its mandate? These are the right questions. Not: "What's the return over the past 12 months?"

This also highlights the value of investment policy statements and pre-committed rules. Writing down, in advance, the criteria by which you will add, reduce, or exit a fund forces clarity. It inoculates against impulsive shifts based on recent performance. Similarly, setting up periodic reviews—say annually, not quarterly—reduces the noise and allows longer-term patterns to emerge. *What feels like stagnation in six months often looks like resilience in five years.*

None of this is easy. Behavioural discipline is the hardest part of investing, precisely because it involves ignoring what feels urgent. But the payoff is substantial. A patient investor who avoids chasing performance doesn't just earn higher returns. They earn compounding's full reward: uninterrupted growth.

There is also a deeper philosophical point. Performance chasing reflects a mindset of control—*if only I choose the right fund at the right time, I can beat the system.* But markets don't reward control. They reward humility, alignment, and staying power. Investors who internalise this understand that the real edge is not in timing markets but in *refusing to be timed by them.*

In closing, the data is clear, the psychology is repeatable, and the pattern is global. Chasing past performance is one of the most consistent destroyers of investor wealth. Avoiding this temptation doesn't require superhuman insight. It requires awareness, process, and the maturity to let time do its work. The next time a glossy chart tempts you to switch funds, remember: *the returns you see may not be the ones you get.*

How to Evaluate an Active Fund Strategically:

Evaluating an active fund is less about finding a star and more about understanding a system. Investors often fall into the trap of selecting funds based on recent outperformance, charismatic managers, or marketing gloss. But superior fund selection is not an act of inspiration—it is a process of discipline. Beneath every outperforming fund is a constellation of decisions, patterns, and costs. The objective isn't simply to find a "good" fund. It is to identify a fund that *delivers more than it costs*, and does so *in a way that aligns with your long-term goals.* To do this, we must examine four critical dimensions: cost, consistency, conviction, and context.

Start with cost, not as a footnote, but as a filter. Active management is expensive by design. There are analyst teams to pay, trades to execute, and overheads to sustain. But price is only a problem when it exceeds value. What matters is *whether the fund's skill justifies the fee.* In practice, very few do. Research from the Financial Conduct Authority (FCA) and global institutions like Morningstar shows that, over long time horizons, most active funds underperform their benchmarks net of fees. This isn't always due to incompetence—it's often the cumulative drag of costs that compounds year after year. Even a difference of 0.50% in annual expenses can erode tens of thousands of pounds over a multi-decade investment period. *If you're paying extra, demand extra—measurable, repeatable, risk-adjusted outperformance.*

But one good year means nothing. Which brings us to consistency. Active funds are not judged by how high they soar in a single cycle, but by how *reliably* they deliver over time. This does not mean they must outperform every year—no fund does. It means they must behave in a way that reflects a disciplined, repeatable process. Examine rolling returns over three-, five-, and ten-year periods. Look for how the fund behaves in different market environments: does it defend well in downturns? Does it participate meaningfully in upswings? Is the outperformance driven by exposure to specific sectors, styles, or just lucky bets? A fund that occasionally wins big but fails to maintain process discipline may be indistinguishable from chance. *Consistency is not glamourous, but in active management, it is one of the most underappreciated sources of alpha.*

Third, assess conviction. This is where qualitative judgment becomes indispensable. Conviction is evident in how a manager constructs the portfolio. Are the top holdings meaningfully weighted? Is the strategy focused or scattered? Are positions held through volatility, or rotated frequently in response to headlines? High-conviction managers often run concentrated portfolios—20 to 40 holdings—where each position carries real weight. They speak with clarity about why they own what they do, and they are willing to be out of step with consensus if their research demands it. Low-conviction funds, by contrast, tend to "hug the benchmark"—owning similar stocks in similar proportions to the index, but charging active fees for passive behaviour. This is often a defensive posture, driven by career risk rather than insight. *True conviction may look uncomfortable in the short term, but it is one of the clearest markers of skill over luck.*

And finally, context. No fund exists in a vacuum. Its merits must be judged not just on performance but on *fit*. Fit with your broader portfolio, fit with your risk appetite, and fit with the current and foreseeable market regime. For instance, a highly active emerging market fund might offer genuine alpha potential—but is it the right tool for a retiree's income portfolio? A small cap deep value strategy might be compelling, but is it appropriate in a tightening credit cycle? Even the best fund can become a misfit when detached from personal context. It's also worth understanding the market efficiency of the fund's domain. Active management tends to work better in less efficient markets—such as small-cap equities, frontier markets, or niche credit strategies—where information is scarcer and pricing anomalies more common. In contrast, large-cap developed markets are ruthlessly efficient. *Paying active fees to compete against algorithms, hedge funds, and billion-dollar quant models often leads to underwhelming outcomes.*

To integrate these factors—cost, consistency, conviction, and context—requires both quantitative scrutiny and qualitative judgement. For example, a fund may charge a relatively high fee (cost) but deliver strong rolling outperformance (consistency), have a tight portfolio of differentiated positions (conviction), and operate in a market segment where active insight can still thrive (context). That fund may well deserve its place in a thoughtful investor's portfolio. Conversely, a fund with middling returns, benchmark-like holdings, high expenses, and vague articulation of strategy should raise red flags, no matter how many awards it's won or how many times it appears on top-performer lists.

It's also worth resisting hype cycles. Funds that suddenly become popular after a spurt of outperformance often underdeliver going forward. By the time a fund makes the headlines, its best ideas may have already played out—and its asset base may have ballooned beyond what the manager can nimbly allocate. The paradox of active investing is that *the more successful a fund becomes, the harder it is to remain exceptional.* Assets scale, opportunities shrink, and incentives tilt toward asset gathering rather than alpha generation.

So how does an intelligent investor navigate the fog of active fund marketing, ratings systems, and noise? Begin by doing what few others do: slow down. Study the fund's full factsheet—not just its recent returns. Read the manager's commentary over multiple quarters. Examine turnover rates, sector allocations, and risk-adjusted metrics like Sharpe ratio or information ratio. Don't just ask, "How much did this fund make?" Ask, "How did it make it? At what risk? With what discipline? In what conditions? And could it do it again?"

There's also merit in understanding the culture of the fund house. Is it driven by a single charismatic manager, or supported by a stable team? Does the firm reward long-term thinking or short-term performance? Are managers incentivised to hold their own funds? Is there skin in the game? These intangible factors can provide early clues about how a fund might behave when the market turns volatile or the spotlight fades. *Culture, while hard to quantify, often trumps strategy when stress arrives.*

Evaluating an active fund is not about predicting the future—it's about understanding the process. The best investors don't pick funds by chasing headlines. They select them by asking grounded, rigorous, and often unglamorous questions. Questions that get beneath the performance and into the engine room. They know that what matters is not only *what* a fund delivers, but *how* and *why*.

In a world saturated with product choice, the investor's edge lies not in finding something novel, but in developing a repeatable framework for discernment. Cost. Consistency. Conviction. Context. Four pillars that, when used with clarity and care, can transform fund selection from a guessing game into a strategy.

Chapter 6
SIPs and the Psychology of Progress

The most potent investment strategy for the everyday investor is rarely flashy, expensive, or complex. Its strength lies in consistency. A Systematic Investment Plan—commonly known as a SIP—is more than a method of regular investing. At its best, it acts as a behavioural framework, guiding us past instinctual mistakes and reinforcing disciplined habits. SIPs work not because markets are predictable, but because humans are not. They transform progress into practice and turn investing into something akin to self-respect rather than speculation.

The principle behind a SIP is elegantly simple: contribute a fixed sum into a chosen mutual fund at set intervals, typically monthly. Yet the true brilliance lies beyond the arithmetic. Its innovation is psychological. A SIP imposes structure in an environment defined by unpredictability and rhythm in a space characterised by noise. For many investors—especially those juggling work, family, and mental bandwidth—a SIP is not merely a tool; it becomes a philosophy.

To appreciate why SIPs work, one must first acknowledge the clash between human nature and financial markets. We are wired for loss aversion, immediate gratification, and emotional overreaction. We vividly remember downturns, crave certainty, and often mistake activity for progress. Markets, by contrast, operate probabilistically, cycle unpredictably, and reward patience over action. SIPs bridge this gap, reducing decision fatigue, dulling the sting of volatility, and quietly training us in the discipline of detachment.

A frequently overlooked advantage is how SIPs neutralise market timing. The aspiration of "buy low, sell high" is rarely realised in practice. Investors are prone to chase rallies and flee after declines, creating a behavioural performance gap: the persistent underperformance of actual investors relative to the funds they hold. SIPs break this destructive loop. Contributions continue automatically, even in moments of fear, generating a form of dollar-cost averaging. This effect is not purely numerical—it is emotional.

Dips are no longer threats; they become opportunities. That shift alone can transform financial futures.

SIPs also instil habit. Investing stops being an act of occasional willpower and becomes a regular, almost meditative practice. Small, visible wins—the accumulation of units, even incrementally—reinforce motivation. Behavioural finance research emphasises that tangible feedback fosters sustained commitment. Over time, SIPs cultivate a financial identity: not merely someone who intends to invest, but someone who acts, reliably and automatically. Repetition sculpts character as much as capital.

The real-world implications are striking. Consider a professional investing ₹5,000 monthly in a balanced mutual fund. Initial market dips induce anxiety. Yet contributions continue, steadily. By year three, average costs are lower, units have accumulated, and apprehension shifts to curiosity. By year five, pride emerges. The individual no longer obsessively monitors NAVs; instead, attention turns to enhancing contributions. This is not luck or insight—it is the quiet effect of automation and time. SIPs do not simply build wealth; they reshape the investor's relationship with money.

Over time, SIPs evolve from routine to ritual. This distinction is subtle but meaningful. Routines are mechanical; rituals carry significance. For many, monthly investing becomes a declaration of agency—a commitment to the future self. It can be the first experience of genuine financial control or a way to heal inherited anxieties around scarcity. Money, after all, is never just arithmetic. It is layered with history, emotion, and psychology. SIPs do not erase these dimensions; they soften them, offering a disciplined act that endures amid noise and turmoil.

Design matters. A SIP that is overly aggressive may generate stress during downturns; one that is too modest may fail to build momentum. The architecture must align with both cash flow and emotional capacity. What can be committed without obsessive monitoring? What sum can persist through income shocks? Which fund truly reflects risk tolerance? These are not technical queries—they are introspective ones. The ideal SIP is not the largest affordable contribution, but the sum that can be sustained quietly over years.

SIPs also democratise investing. Before their advent, mutual funds seemed exclusive, arcane, and administratively cumbersome. SIPs transformed accessibility: low minimums, online platforms, minimal paperwork. Participation is no longer determined by wealth but by willingness. This shift matters profoundly, inviting younger, irregular-income, or first-time investors to take part. Progress becomes attainable, not aspirational.

As economic uncertainty grows and public pensions strain, personal investing will only gain importance. Strategies that work with human behaviour, rather than against it, endure. SIPs do not promise market-beating returns; they promise behavioural fidelity. And in the long arc of wealth creation, disciplined behaviour is often the single greatest differentiator.

This chapter will unpack SIPs in full—the financial mechanics, the cognitive patterns, the emotional reinforcement. You will learn how SIPs counteract impulsive timing, cultivate identity through repetition, and integrate into lives with unpredictable cash flows and shifting moods. You will also gain tools to construct a SIP that feels like progress, not obligation: an act of design, not mere performance.

The true power of a SIP is not measured by market impact, but by its influence on the investor. It fosters a durable conviction that the future is worth funding—consistently, quietly, and without drama.

What a SIP Really Does to Your Brain

If you were to design a financial tool specifically to counter the most destructive instincts of the human mind, it would look strikingly similar to a Systematic Investment Plan. That's not coincidence. The SIP, often described in dry, procedural terms—automated monthly deductions into a mutual fund—is, in fact, one of the few financial structures that actively works with human psychology instead of against it. It doesn't rely on perfect knowledge, perfect timing, or even perfect discipline. It relies on *rhythm*. And in doing so, it bypasses much of the mental noise that undermines long-term financial success.

The modern investor faces a paradox. We have more information than ever before, but greater anxiety. More tools, but less confidence. Greater market access, but weaker behaviour. Much of this comes down to how our brains are wired. The human mind evolved in environments of scarcity and danger, not abundance and delayed gratification. We respond more strongly to losses than to gains, obsess over short-term fluctuations, and panic in the face of uncertainty—even when we *know*, rationally, that volatility is the price of long-term reward. This is where the SIP becomes a behavioural intervention as much as a financial strategy.

The brilliance of the SIP lies in how it bypasses emotional interference. By automating investing at fixed intervals—typically monthly—it removes the single most damaging variable in investing: *timing decisions driven by mood, media, or market noise.* When you set up a SIP, you're effectively saying, "I don't trust myself to make 12 rational decisions a year—but I do trust myself to make one good one and automate the rest." This may sound modest, even unambitious. But behavioural research suggests it's exactly this sort of self-aware simplicity that works. *SIPs reduce decision fatigue, and with it, decision regret.*

To appreciate how deeply SIPs affect the brain, one must understand the mechanics of mental energy. Every decision we make—whether to invest, to hold, to panic, to switch funds—draws on a finite reservoir of cognitive resources. In psychology, this is called ego depletion. The more decisions you force yourself to make, especially under stress, the worse your subsequent choices become. SIPs, by removing the need for constant re-evaluation, preserve mental energy for the things that actually require it—like planning, earning, or learning. *They protect attention spans in a world that monetises distraction.*

SIPs also gamify investing in a subtle, effective way. Each contribution becomes a measurable win. The regularity of seeing new units added to one's portfolio offers a form of micro-reward—a dopamine feedback loop not unlike exercise tracking or habit streaks. Importantly, it's progress you can see, not just hope for. Over time, these visible reinforcements help build financial confidence, replacing the anxiety of market watching with the calm of contribution. Instead of wondering what the market will do next, the investor begins to focus on what they can control: participation.

This behavioural conditioning is not trivial. It reshapes identity. Investors who engage in SIPs over long periods often report a shift in self-perception. They stop seeing themselves as outsiders to finance and start identifying as someone who *invests*. This is significant because identity precedes habit durability. We are more likely to sustain behaviours that align with our self-image. The person who thinks, "I am the kind of person who builds wealth every month, no matter what the market does," is more resilient in downturns and less susceptible to hype during bull runs. *SIPs do not just change outcomes—they change people.*

At the neurological level, SIPs counteract the limbic system's impulse to react to short-term threat. Market crashes, negative headlines, portfolio red—these all trigger stress responses akin to physical danger. Cortisol spikes, the prefrontal cortex narrows, and fight-or-flight kicks in. The rational mind, responsible for weighing risk and time horizons, is sidelined. What the SIP does is inoculate the investor against this hijack. By automating a response *in advance*, it reduces the temptation to react *in the moment*. The investor doesn't need to override panic—they simply bypass it. *This is not willpower; it is design.*

Real-world data confirms the power of this approach. Studies comparing investor returns to fund returns consistently show a "behaviour gap"—the difference between what funds earned and what investors took home, largely due to poor timing decisions. Morningstar's analysis, for instance, shows that investors in volatile funds often underperform the funds themselves by up to 1–2% annually, simply because of erratic entry and exit patterns. SIPs, by enforcing disciplined entry regardless of market conditions, close this gap. They align investor experience with fund performance.

But the benefits are not only defensive. SIPs also offer a pathway to proactive, empowering financial planning. They enable investors to align cash flows with long-term goals in a granular, manageable way. Rather than waiting to accumulate a large lump sum—a daunting task for most—SIPs allow individuals to *start now, start small, and scale later.* This immediacy is psychologically powerful. It transforms investing from a distant aspiration into a present-tense activity. And because contributions are spread out, the emotional stakes of any single market movement are lowered. *It becomes easier to invest when your brain doesn't feel like every decision could ruin you.*

This is especially relevant in volatile or declining markets. While lump-sum investors tend to freeze or flee in downturns, SIP investors often benefit from falling prices through the mechanics of rupee-cost averaging. Lower prices mean more units bought per rupee. Over time, this reduces average cost per unit and enhances long-term returns—if, and only if, the investor *keeps going.* This "if" is psychological, not financial. And SIPs increase the odds of endurance by reducing friction. They make *staying invested feel easier than opting out.*

The emotional arc of SIP investing is also worth noting. The first year often feels thankless—contributions seem small, returns modest, and market moves confusing. But by year three or five, something shifts. Compound interest begins to show itself. Not spectacularly, but steadily. Investors see growth that exceeds their inputs, reinforcing the sense that their quiet commitment is working. That sense—*of participating in something larger, slower, and more reliable than daily market drama*—can be incredibly grounding. It builds trust not just in markets, but in one's own process.

Of course, no tool is perfect. SIPs don't eliminate risk, nor do they guarantee returns. Poor fund selection, over-aggressive allocations, or misalignment with life stage can all dilute their power. But when implemented thoughtfully—aligned with personal goals, cash flows, and tolerance for volatility—SIPs represent a rare blend of financial prudence and psychological sustainability. *They are not glamorous, but they are enduring.*

There is something almost subversive about this. In a world that glorifies action, speed, and hot tips, the SIP whispers a different message: "Progress is cumulative. Stay the course." It rewards consistency over cleverness, humility over heroism. And for many investors, that's not just a financial lesson—it's a philosophical one.

As we examine SIPs more deeply through this chapter, keep this framing in mind: *they are not simply about automation—they are about alignment.* With your values, your limits, your long-term aspirations. And when viewed through the lens of behavioural science, the humble SIP emerges not as a mechanical utility, but as a behavioural design innovation—a way of tricking ourselves into doing the right thing, again and again, until it no longer feels like effort. It just feels like life.

The Antidote to Market Timing

The problem with market timing is not simply that it fails. It's that it seduces. Investors—amateurs and professionals alike—are irresistibly drawn to the illusion that with enough data, intuition, or boldness, one can buy low and sell high with precision. The human brain craves patterns, narratives, and agency, especially in environments of uncertainty. Markets offer just enough feedback to fuel the illusion of control. Yet history is unambiguous: even the most sophisticated investors consistently struggle to outguess the market's twists and turns. Systematic Investment Plans (SIPs), when properly understood, offer not just a practical countermeasure—they represent a cognitive breakthrough. They free us from a behavioural trap that has eroded more wealth than poor returns ever did.

Market timing, at its core, is an emotional decision disguised as a rational one. The investor tells themselves they are "waiting for a better entry point" or "locking in gains" out of prudence, but what often underlies these choices is fear—fear of missing out, fear of loss, fear of regret. SIPs interrupt this cycle by removing the decision-making moment altogether. They transform investing from a series of emotionally charged events into a calm, rule-based routine. Every month, the same amount is invested, regardless of headlines, predictions, or market noise. Over time, this regularity creates a powerful advantage: it decouples action from emotion. The investor participates in the market's growth without having to endure its daily theatre.

The concept behind SIPs is elegantly simple. By investing the same amount at regular intervals, one naturally buys more units when prices are low and fewer when prices are high. This phenomenon, known as rupee-cost averaging, doesn't guarantee superior returns, but it does offer behavioural insulation. It prevents investors from doing the one thing that nearly always destroys long-term performance—selling low and buying high. Numerous studies confirm this. Morningstar's "Investor Return" studies repeatedly show that the average investor underperforms their own investments. Why? Because they tend to enter after strong performance and exit during downturns. SIPs are a direct antidote to this performance-chasing impulse. They eliminate the temptation to time the market because they remove the choice.

There is something profoundly countercultural about this. In nearly every other domain—business, education, sport—agility, responsiveness, and selective timing are signs of mastery. But investing punishes activity. Vanguard founder John Bogle famously said, "Don't do something—just stand there." SIPs are a disciplined application of that paradox. By automating the decision to invest and committing to regular contributions, investors shift the source of edge from prediction to consistency. *It's not about having the perfect insight once—it's about having the right behaviour repeatedly.*

The effect is not merely financial. It is psychological. When investors move from discretionary, sporadic investing to structured SIPs, they often report a shift in mindset. Volatility becomes less threatening because they know they are buying more when prices dip. Downturns, instead of provoking anxiety, start to feel like opportunities. The emotional burden of "when should I invest?" is replaced by the quiet confidence of "I already did." Over time, this turns investing into a stabilising force rather than a source of stress.

Consider a visual thought experiment. Imagine two investors starting in January 2008—just before the global financial crisis. One invests a lump sum of ₹1,20,000. The other invests ₹10,000 every month for 12 months through a SIP. By the end of the year, the SIP investor will have endured the same brutal headlines and market declines, yet their average cost per unit will be lower. When markets recover—as they tend to do—the SIP investor's portfolio regains ground faster. More importantly, the SIP investor is far less likely to have bailed out at the bottom, because their investment was not a one-time emotional commitment. It was a habit.

The power of SIPs lies not in market-beating returns, but in investor-beating behaviour. That's a distinction often missed. It's not that SIPs are some magical return-enhancing mechanism. Rather, they succeed by neutralising the investor's worst instincts. Over decades, this discipline quietly compounds. It avoids the common pitfall of missing the market's best days, which often cluster around the worst. As one analysis from JP Morgan showed, missing just the 10 best days in the S&P 500 over a 20-year period could cut an investor's return in half. Yet these best days often occur within weeks of major crashes—precisely when most investors are sitting on the sidelines, licking their wounds, or waiting for "clarity."

Clarity, of course, is a myth. Markets never announce turning points. They shift suddenly, often amid pessimism. SIPs don't wait for certainty—they operate through it. *That's their genius.* Investors using SIPs never need to guess whether the market is overvalued, undervalued, or entering a new regime. They simply show up. Month after month, year after year. Over a decade or two, that consistency becomes destiny.

This isn't to suggest that SIPs are immune to scrutiny. Timing still matters when one begins the SIP, and not all markets reward this strategy equally. But over long horizons, particularly in growth-oriented economies like India's, the SIP framework aligns beautifully with structural trends. It harnesses the natural upward drift of equity markets while smoothing out the chaos in between. For younger investors or those building wealth gradually, it is arguably the most rational approach available—not because it maximises every rupee invested, but because it maximises the investor's ability to stay the course.

Ironically, the longer one practices SIP investing, the more detached one becomes from the day-to-day pulse of the market. That detachment is a feature, not a flaw. In behavioural finance, success is often measured not by returns, but by regret minimisation. SIPs minimise regret by avoiding binary decisions. There is no haunting memory of "if only I had waited." There is only the slow, rhythmic progress of contributions compounding. Over time, this builds a deeper kind of confidence—one rooted not in prediction, but in process.

And it's this process that allows the investor to achieve what might be called *dollar-cost zen*: a mental state where markets no longer dictate mood, where volatility ceases to induce panic, and where investing becomes not a reaction to news but an act of discipline. It is the peace of knowing that no matter what the headlines scream, your system is quietly at work, moving you forward.

For many investors, especially those juggling demanding careers, families, and financial obligations, the SIP becomes more than just an investment strategy. It becomes a form of mental hygiene. A way to outsource willpower and turn sporadic intent into sustained action. Like brushing one's teeth or going for a walk, it becomes embedded in routine—and in doing so, liberates mental energy for more meaningful pursuits.

Ultimately, SIPs offer a profound shift: from being reactive to being intentional. From hoping to acting. From chasing performance to building wealth. In a world that rewards noise, the quiet, automated rhythm of a SIP is its own kind of rebellion. And like most rebellions, it is only understood in hindsight—when others are wondering how you got so far with so little drama.

SIP as Ritual, Not Routine

Most people think of a Systematic Investment Plan (SIP) as a financial mechanism—an automatic debit from a bank account into a mutual fund. On paper, that's all it is. But to reduce it to mere automation is to miss its deeper potential. For the financially anxious, the overcommitted, or the quietly overwhelmed, SIPs can become far more than a transaction. They can evolve into a ritual—a monthly declaration of self-worth, discipline, and belief in a future that doesn't yet exist. When reimagined in this way, SIPs cease to be administrative tasks and begin to function as acts of emotional resilience.

To understand this transformation, one must first grasp what financial anxiety does to the mind. It creates fragmentation. Unpaid bills, uncertain savings, unpredictable expenses—these aren't just line items. They are sources of chronic stress, often simmering below conscious awareness, shaping behaviours in subtle but destructive ways. Procrastination, compulsive spending, avoidance of financial planning—these habits aren't rooted in laziness or ignorance, but in fear. SIPs offer a way out, not just because they allocate money, but because they simplify choice. They create one clear, recurring action that pushes back against chaos. *In a world full of variables, they offer a fixed point of progress.*

Consider Aarti, a 34-year-old media professional in Mumbai. For years, she avoided investing altogether. Despite earning well, she never felt confident about markets and often felt guilty for her lack of "financial literacy." Her bank balance would surge after salary day and dwindle before month-end—always reactive, never deliberate. When a friend suggested SIPs, she resisted. "I don't want to lock up my money. What if I need it?" she asked. But eventually, she set up a modest monthly SIP—₹3,000 into a balanced hybrid fund. Within three months, something shifted. It wasn't just her balance sheet that looked different—it was her internal narrative. She had taken agency. That single action began to erode the shame she'd carried for years about "not doing enough." She wasn't trying to master the markets. She was trying to regain trust in herself. *The SIP wasn't about growing wealth. It was about growing confidence.*

There is a profound psychological difference between a task and a ritual. A task is something to be completed. A ritual is something that completes you. Tasks generate fatigue. Rituals generate meaning. When a SIP is anchored in values rather than performance—when it becomes a monthly act of alignment with one's goals and identity—it begins to reshape the investor. It acts as a behavioural anchor, reinforcing the belief that the future matters, that one is capable of consistency, and that small, repeated actions have power. This is especially valuable in a world addicted to quick wins and short-term dopamine.

Financial systems rarely acknowledge the emotional and narrative dimension of money. Products are designed to optimise returns, not reduce shame. Advisors are trained to build portfolios, not self-worth. But the data is clear: most people don't underperform the market—they underperform themselves. They abandon good strategies because they feel overwhelmed, uncertain, or out of control. SIPs interrupt this pattern. They reduce the frequency of decision-making and thus the likelihood of error. But more importantly, they reduce the emotional volatility that drives those errors in the first place. *They quiet the internal noise that says: you're behind, you're not doing enough, you don't understand.*

Rituals also create a rhythm. And rhythm is how humans experience time. Without rituals, life becomes a blur of unrelated events. With them, it becomes a pattern. SIPs—when done mindfully—can restore this sense of pattern. On the 5th of every month, a tiny act of commitment takes place. You might not see the result for years, but you know it's accumulating. You begin to trust the invisible. This trust, once built, bleeds into other areas of life. You start meal prepping more often. You follow through on that book you meant to finish. *Discipline, once seeded in one domain, tends to grow roots elsewhere.*

It's also worth noting that SIPs remove the need for performance theatre. You don't need to talk about "hot stocks" or forecast the next big economic trend. You don't have to be clever. You just have to be consistent. This is especially liberating in social environments where financial bravado often masquerades as wisdom. For many women, younger professionals, or those from non-finance backgrounds, the world of investing can feel alienating. SIPs offer an alternative path—not through technical expertise but through behavioural alignment. No jargon required. No ego involved.

Let's return to the idea of self-respect. Most people associate it with assertiveness, boundaries, or confidence. But at its core, self-respect is built through self-honouring behaviours. Every time you keep a promise to yourself—however small—you reinforce your sense of worth. SIPs are micro-promises. They don't require mood, motivation, or willpower once they're in place. They just need follow-through. And each month they follow through on your behalf. *That's where their quiet genius lies.*

There are of course criticisms. Some argue that SIPs don't optimise for returns, especially in trending markets. Others say that lump sum investing, if timed well, is superior. These are valid in theory but irrelevant in practice for most people. Behavioural errors cost far more than suboptimal allocation. The real enemy is not underperformance—it's inconsistency, abandonment, emotional trading. SIPs win not because they always deliver the highest returns, but because they prevent the costliest mistakes. *In investing, the best tool is often not the most sophisticated, but the one you can actually stick with.*

This behavioural anchoring is especially powerful when visualised. Many SIP platforms now show users a graph of projected corpus growth, month by month, year by year. But the real progress is often invisible. It's in the growing space between stimulus and reaction. It's in the reduced anxiety when markets fall. It's in the confidence that one is not starting from zero every month. Financial health, like physical health, is rarely about perfection. It's about direction.

Another story: Vinod, a 42-year-old tech consultant in Bangalore, had a history of impulsive investing. Every year he'd start strong—diversifying across funds, reading economic reports—but by July he'd pause SIPs, chase new opportunities, or hold back "until the market corrected." Over a decade, he earned less than the funds he chose. Frustrated, he eventually outsourced his investing to a SIP-only model through a robo-advisor. The experience was revelatory. "It was like switching from manual gear to cruise control," he said. "Not as thrilling, but I finally got where I was going." The metaphor stuck. Investing didn't need to be thrilling. It needed to be reliable.

Ultimately, the shift from routine to ritual is a shift from compliance to connection. From obligation to meaning. From financial maintenance to financial dignity. It requires no ceremony, no spiritual overtones—just a reframing of the act. The SIP is not a debit line on a statement. It is a self-made symbol. A whisper to your future self: I'm thinking of you. I'm building something. I haven't forgotten.

And in a culture constantly pressuring us to consume now and worry later, that quiet whisper may be the most radical financial act of all.

How to Set Up a SIP That Actually Fits Your Life

The real success of a Systematic Investment Plan isn't defined by how much you invest—it's determined by how well it fits. Not to a theoretical model, not to what your colleague is doing, and certainly not to some generic rule-of-thumb about saving 20% of your income. It must fit *you.* Your cash flow, your temperament, your anxiety threshold, your long-term needs, and your short-term constraints. Anything less is not just unsustainable; it's counterproductive. The illusion of discipline quickly collapses under the weight of unrealistic expectations. To build a SIP that lasts, you must start with realism, not aspiration.

This is where most people go wrong. They treat SIPs as static commitments rather than dynamic tools. The result is a plan that feels rigid or disconnected from life as it is actually lived. For example, setting up an aggressive ₹20,000 monthly SIP because you read that "more is better" makes sense until your rent rises, a medical expense arrives, or your bonus is delayed. The next thing you know, you pause the SIP "for just a month." That month becomes three. Then you restart. Then you stop again. The stop-start pattern erodes both return and motivation. *Discipline is not a sprint—it is a choreography with life.*

The better approach is to reverse-engineer the SIP from your lived reality. Begin with cash flow. Understand when money enters your account and when it exits. This is not a spreadsheet exercise. It's a mindfulness practice. The goal is to notice your financial rhythms—how they shift through the month, what triggers impulsive spending, where leaks occur. Once you see this clearly, you'll know whether your SIP should be monthly, fortnightly, or even weekly. Some investors find that smaller, more frequent SIPs create a stronger behavioural link to consistency. Others prefer one decisive debit right after payday, turning the SIP into a kind of financial "tithing" before temptation has a chance to strike. There is no universal answer—only the right answer for *your* pattern.

The second dimension is amount. This is not about ambition; it is about sustainability. The right amount is not the maximum you can afford—it's the amount you can afford *without friction.* If you have to rearrange other expenses every month just to keep your SIP alive, the plan is flawed. Overcommitting doesn't signal financial discipline—it signals a misreading of your actual life. The most effective SIPs start comfortably and scale up gradually. Begin with a small but non-trivial amount—something you notice but don't resent. Over time, increase it in sync with income growth, debt reduction, or improved budgeting. These incremental increases have far more impact over decades than dramatic but inconsistent contributions. *Think of SIPs not as events, but as habits that mature with you.*

Fund type is the third—and most misunderstood—variable. Many new investors default to aggressive equity funds, attracted by the promise of high returns over long periods. While that can be appropriate for long-term wealth building, it fails when the investor's emotional risk tolerance is not aligned. The best SIP in the wrong fund becomes a ticking time bomb of regret. As soon as the market falls—and it will—the investor panics, cancels the SIP, and withdraws. All the behavioural value of the SIP is lost. The remedy is to match fund type not just to goal duration, but to your ability to *emotionally tolerate volatility*. If you check your investments weekly, are prone to worry, or have never experienced a downturn, consider starting with hybrid funds or balanced advantage funds. Their returns may be lower, but the cost of emotional churn is far higher. A good SIP is not just about *growth*—it's about *durability*.

This brings us to a rarely discussed insight: your SIP should change with your life stage, not just your income. A 27-year-old with variable freelance income may benefit more from flexible SIPs into debt or low-volatility equity funds, allowing for liquidity and mental ease. A 35-year-old with a stable job and a toddler might choose education-focused equity funds with a 15-year horizon, but split the SIP across two or three funds to hedge volatility. A 50-year-old nearing retirement should probably redirect SIPs into conservative hybrid funds or even short-duration debt funds, reinforcing capital protection. *A SIP is not a product—it is a personal protocol. And protocols must evolve.*

Let's also talk about goals. There's a tendency to set up SIPs in isolation, without clear alignment to specific targets. This is a mistake. An unlabeled SIP becomes abstract. A SIP tied to a tangible outcome—a home down payment in 7 years, a sabbatical in 5, a child's college in 15—becomes sticky. It becomes emotionally charged. This isn't just motivational fluff. Behavioural finance consistently shows that "goal tagging" improves persistence. You are far more likely to continue investing during a downturn if you know *what* you are investing for. It gives the discomfort meaning. It transforms short-term uncertainty into long-term trust.

But don't stop at financial alignment. Consider emotional alignment. If your SIP stresses you out, if it feels like another demand in a life already overloaded, it will eventually be rejected. The key question to ask is: *Does this plan support who I am becoming, or is it a burden I am forcing myself to carry?* A well-designed SIP should *lighten* your mental load, not add to it. It should create a sense of quiet progress—a feeling that, no matter how chaotic the month, one thing moved forward. This feeling compounds, just like returns do. It builds financial confidence at a pace no market can replicate.

Now a word on flexibility. Many investors feel that changing a SIP is a sign of failure. It isn't. Life changes—so should your plan. It's far better to reduce your SIP temporarily than to cancel it altogether. Most mutual fund platforms now allow dynamic SIPs, where the amount can vary based on your chosen formula or inputs. Use these tools. Don't let rigidity become the enemy of sustainability. The key is to avoid overreaction. If you must make a change, do it after reflection, not during emotional peaks or troughs. Build in quarterly reviews where you ask: *Is my SIP still the right size, shape, and style for my life right now?*

Let's end with an often-overlooked but crucial principle: *SIP setup is not a one-time act—it's an ongoing relationship.* It is less like buying a product and more like designing a system that grows with you. The ideal SIP adapts to your income, your responsibilities, your mood swings, and even your missteps. It supports you when you're steady and forgives you when you're stretched. That's what makes it so powerful. It is not just a conduit for capital—it is a reflection of your capacity to commit, adapt, and believe.

In a world obsessed with optimisation, it's tempting to focus on the "best" fund or the "perfect" amount. But the truth is simpler and more profound. The best SIP is not the one that grows the fastest. It is the one you actually continue. The one that survives the bad months. The one you don't abandon when life gets unpredictable. *Consistency always beats complexity.*

If you remember nothing else, remember this: A SIP is not about numbers. It is about trust—trust in your future self, in your system, and in the idea that progress doesn't need drama. Just design it well. Then let it work.

Chapter 7
Risk Isn't What You Think It Is

Most investors aren't paralysed by the mechanics of finance—they're paralysed by fear. Peel back the layers of hesitation, and you find a story not about numbers, but about anxiety: a vague, ambient unease that feeds on half-truths and misperceptions. To navigate markets intelligently, we must confront a persistent misconception: risk is not the same as volatility. A sudden dip, a red day on your portfolio, or a jagged line on a chart—these are merely symptoms. True risk, the kind that quietly erodes financial wellbeing, is far subtler: inaction. Doing nothing, delaying entry, or tiptoeing into the market is far more dangerous than any temporary fluctuation.

This chapter exists to untangle that confusion. Many investors, novice and seasoned alike, inherit a vocabulary of risk that is emotionally charged, intellectually imprecise, and historically outdated. They equate risk with movement, unpredictability, or any threat to their sense of control. But the market does not punish motion; it rewards patience. Volatility does not ruin portfolios—panic does. And panic thrives where comprehension is absent.

Consider this: volatility is not loss. This distinction is not trivial—it is the difference between weather and climate. Weather shifts hourly; climate defines the system over time. Investors who react to every market tremor are like travellers cancelling a trip because of a passing drizzle. Daily swings are noise; long-term structure and growth are the reality. Treating every decline as catastrophic is not vigilance—it is behavioural fragility.

Volatility, in fact, is necessary. It is the price of entry. A perfectly smooth market would offer no reward—no growth, no premium for taking a position. Investing implies accepting short-term discomfort in exchange for long-term gain. The task is not to eliminate risk, but to construct a framework where it is tolerable. The real question is not "how do I avoid risk?" but rather, "what degree of risk can I sustain without undermining my own strategy?"

Time transforms this understanding. Ten- and fifteen-year rolling returns of diversified equity portfolios consistently show positive outcomes. Short-term losses are inevitable; long-term losses are the exception, provided diversification and discipline are maintained. This is empirical, not aspirational. Daily volatility recedes in significance over years, revealing the slow but compounding arc of capital growth. Yet most people are wired for immediacy. Headlines, apps, market alerts—they all whisper: act now. But successful investing is a craft of patience. Holding is not passivity; it is resilience.

The irony is stark: the gravest risk for most investors is not losing money in the market—it is failing to participate at all, or entering timidly, belatedly, with insufficient capital. Inflation does not pause for indecision. Procrastination compounds inversely to interest, eroding not only immediate returns but also the compounding that magnifies them over time. Fear of loss often ensures the very outcome it seeks to avoid: a diminished financial future.

Reframing risk is therefore essential. Risk is not inherently harmful—it is uncertainty. And uncertainty is an inescapable fact of life, not a flaw in the market. The goal is not a mythical "zero-risk" path. There is none. The goal is to identify your personal risk zone—a space where your financial plan aligns with both your goals and your temperament, where you can remain invested through downturns, confusing cycles, and inevitable noise.

Finding that zone requires self-awareness, not bravado. Later in the chapter, we'll explore a simple diagnostic framework to assess risk identity. Are you a "strategic tortoise," prioritising stability and peace of mind? A "pragmatic lion," capable of weathering volatility with a clear long-term vision? Or a "guarded owl," cautious yet consistent when supported by structure? Each persona aligns with different fund types, asset allocations, and behavioural practices. The objective is not to select the "best" approach—it is to select the one that fits you, and then reinforce it with discipline.

We must also dismantle the mythology that complexity equals safety. Many investors are lured by products promising low risk through exotic structures—hedge funds, structured notes, derivatives wrapped in opaque packaging. Visible volatility may diminish, but invisible complexity grows. Complexity that is hidden is dangerous: difficult to understand, hard to exit, and easy to misprice. By contrast, simple investments—broad index funds, balanced hybrid funds, diversified equity portfolios—are not simplistic. They are transparent. And transparency remains the most effective safeguard against risk.

Fear, too, must be addressed honestly. It is a natural response to uncertainty. But if fear is your default lens, perception becomes distorted. Every correction appears catastrophic. Every bear market signals systemic failure. Every cautionary article seems a directive to sell. This is not risk awareness—it is fear masquerading as prudence, and it costs far more than any financial loss ever could.

Developing genuine risk intelligence means holding two truths simultaneously: markets will fall, and you will endure if prepared. Achieving this requires emotional infrastructure as much as financial tools. Systems that keep you steady when instincts urge panic—SIPs, strategic asset allocation, pre-commitment devices—serve as behavioural scaffolds. They shield you from the impulses that sabotage long-term outcomes.

This chapter guides you in constructing that scaffolding deliberately. You will explore how volatility functions, how time transforms its significance, and how the most insidious risks are often disguised as safety. You will learn to design investments not around market moods, but around your own capacity for consistency. By the end, your risk philosophy will be grounded in evidence, aligned with your temperament, and resilient enough to endure reality.

Risk does not bend to perception. But once you understand its true nature—what it costs, what it offers, and how it behaves—you can cease fearing it, begin managing it, and, ultimately, make progress that endures.

Volatility vs Loss: Know the Difference

Few things in investing are more misunderstood than the concept of volatility. For many, it is seen as a red flag, a warning, a sign that something has gone wrong. A sharp fall in the value of a fund or index provokes anxiety, headlines, and sometimes rash decisions. But to treat volatility as equivalent to loss is not just mistaken—it's hazardous. It conflates temporary fluctuation with permanent damage, leading investors to act on fear rather than reason. The antidote begins with a clear distinction: *volatility is movement; loss is finality*. One is a feature of markets; the other is a result of behaviour.

The analogy of weather versus climate is particularly useful here. Weather is unpredictable, often inconvenient, and sometimes extreme. It changes by the hour. But it tells you little about the overall pattern. Climate, by contrast, is stable, directional, and built on data across decades. To panic about volatility is like abandoning a walking tour because it rained once. You're reacting to a local event without understanding the broader trend. The same applies to financial markets. Daily or even annual swings in price are not indicators of failure; they are the cost of admission to long-term reward.

To see this distinction more clearly, consider the historical behaviour of equity markets. Over any given day, the odds of a positive return are roughly 54%. Not much better than a coin toss. But stretch that window to one year, and the odds improve to around 70%. Extend it to ten years, and they rise to over 90%. The message is simple but powerful: *the longer you stay invested, the lower your chance of experiencing actual loss*. Volatility flattens with time. Its sting is softened by patience.

Yet this truth often fails to penetrate when fear takes hold. That's because investors don't just process markets intellectually—they experience them emotionally. And emotionally, a drop in value feels the same whether it's temporary or permanent. Behavioural finance research has consistently shown that losses are felt more intensely than equivalent gains. A 10% decline hurts more than a 10% rise feels good. This asymmetry drives poor decisions: selling low, buying high, abandoning strategy. In many cases, the real damage is not done by the market at all—it is inflicted by the investor's reaction to volatility, not the volatility itself.

What, then, is the role of volatility? Why do we tolerate it? Because without it, return would not exist. Volatility is the reflection of risk, and risk is the engine of growth. Safe assets—such as savings accounts or government bonds—offer stability precisely because they offer so little in return. The possibility of loss is what creates the opportunity for gain. If a market never moved down, it could never move up either. This is why volatility should be seen not as a danger to avoid, but as a signal that the system is working. *It is the discomfort that makes the comfort of compounding possible.*

To illustrate the difference between volatility and loss in practical terms, consider two investors. Both put £10,000 into the same equity fund. One checks their account weekly, reacts to every dip, and exits after a 15% drop, converting a paper decline into a realised loss. The other stays put, ignoring the noise. Five years later, the fund recovers and compounds to £15,000. Both experienced the same volatility. Only one experienced loss. The lesson is clear: *volatility is inevitable; loss is optional.*

This understanding should influence how we design portfolios. Asset allocation is not just about maximising return—it's about calibrating volatility to the investor's temperament and time horizon. A young professional with a 30-year horizon can afford more equity exposure than a retiree drawing down capital. But more importantly, the younger investor must be taught *why* the volatility they'll encounter is not a threat. It's not enough to hand someone a diversified portfolio. You must also equip them with the emotional tools to endure the very cycles that make the strategy work.

One of the most effective tools in this regard is the concept of dollar-cost averaging, or its British equivalent in Systematic Investment Plans (SIPs). By investing a fixed amount regularly, regardless of market conditions, investors are able to buy more units when prices are low and fewer when prices are high. Over time, this smooths out the impact of volatility and turns market dips into opportunities rather than threats. But beyond the maths, SIPs work because they reframe volatility. Instead of fearing the dip, the disciplined investor welcomes it—knowing it improves long-term returns.

Let's also confront the cultural component. Financial media thrives on the drama of volatility. "Markets Crash!" is more clickable than "Long-Term Trends Intact." This skews public perception. A 3% drop is presented with the same urgency as a structural collapse. But markets have always been volatile. Since the early 20th century, the S&P 500 has experienced an average intra-year drop of nearly 14%, yet ended the year higher more often than not. Volatility is not news. It's normal.

Of course, not all volatility is benign. When volatility signals deeper structural risk—such as unsustainable leverage, fraud, or broken business models—it can precede genuine loss. But these cases are the exception, not the rule. The vast majority of daily price movement reflects sentiment, speculation, and liquidity—not fundamental decline. *Knowing when volatility matters—and when it doesn't—is a critical mark of investing maturity.*

One of the most dangerous investor behaviours is extrapolation. A down week feels like it will become a down month, a down year. But the data doesn't support this. Market timing based on short-term signals has a terrible track record. DALBAR studies consistently show that the average investor underperforms the very funds they invest in—because they enter and exit at the wrong times, usually driven by volatility-induced fear. This behaviour converts what should have been temporary into something permanent. *Volatility is not your enemy. Reacting poorly to it is.*

The way forward is not to eliminate volatility, but to internalise it. To accept it as part of the process. This requires education, reflection, and a redefinition of risk itself. Risk is not fluctuation. It is the possibility that your money will not be there when you need it. That could come from market loss—but it could just as easily come from inflation, underinvestment, or poor timing. Once we expand our definition of risk, volatility starts to look less like a villain and more like a messenger.

Emotional resilience is therefore the greatest asset a long-term investor can cultivate. This doesn't mean ignoring discomfort—it means not obeying it. The best investors are not the ones who predict the future. They are the ones who can sit through uncertainty without abandoning their plan. And that ability starts with understanding what volatility *is* and, more importantly, what it *isn't*.

Volatility is not the same as failure. It is not proof that you were wrong, or that the market is broken, or that your plan needs a reboot. It is the normal, sometimes jarring, but ultimately harmless process by which real returns are delivered. Confusing it with loss is like confusing turbulence with a plane crash. Both may shake you—but only one ends your journey.

The responsibility of the modern investor is to stay educated, stay calm, and stay invested. If you can learn to treat volatility as a signal rather than a verdict, you'll not only survive the markets—you'll give yourself a genuine edge. Because while most investors are trying to escape the discomfort, you'll understand it. And *that*, more than any algorithm or insider tip, is the real secret to long-term success.

Time as the Great Risk Reducer

Risk is one of the most misunderstood concepts in investing—not because it is elusive, but because it is so often framed in isolation from time. The moment an investor hears the word "risk," they instinctively picture loss: sharp declines, wiped-out capital, catastrophic crashes. But risk is not simply the probability of something bad happening. In investing, *risk is contextual.* And perhaps the most powerful context for redefining risk is time. The longer your investment horizon, the more risk becomes a transient illusion rather than a real threat. Put differently: *time doesn't eliminate risk—but it changes its shape.*

To understand this, we need to step away from the daily financial headlines and consider long-term data. If you invested in equities on any single day in the past century, your odds of seeing a positive return one year later were only modestly better than a coin toss. But stretch that to ten years, and your odds improve significantly. Over twenty years, the historical data becomes almost unanimous: long-term equity investors who stayed the course overwhelmingly ended up with gains—not despite volatility, but because they endured it. This is not conjecture. It is the cumulative verdict of market history.

Consider the S&P 500, often used as a proxy for U.S. equity markets. Since its inception, it has delivered average annualised returns of roughly 10%, despite dozens of recessions, crashes, geopolitical crises, and pandemics. But that number tells only part of the story. When you zoom in, the path is anything but smooth—steep climbs followed by jarring drops. For investors with a short time horizon, these drops can feel unbearable. But for those with a twenty- or thirty-year horizon, these events become statistical noise. *What matters is not the path's jaggedness, but its direction.*

This is not to say that time automatically guarantees positive outcomes. Timing still matters, and poor decisions—like panic-selling or over-concentration—can derail even long horizons. But the broader point stands: *market volatility compresses over time.* The dispersion of possible outcomes narrows. Short-term results are dominated by randomness and emotion. Long-term outcomes, however, are shaped by earnings growth, reinvestment, and macroeconomic resilience.

A useful analogy comes from physics: the concept of signal-to-noise ratio. In the short term, markets are mostly noise—daily fluctuations driven by sentiment, media narratives, algorithmic trades. But over the long term, the signal emerges: the real progress of businesses, the compounding of dividends, the expansion of economies. Time is the filter that helps us separate signal from noise. Without it, investors are flying blind through static.

Yet many investors continue to behave as if time is irrelevant. They check their portfolios daily, react to news cycles, and judge performance over months rather than decades. This short-termism is not merely unhelpful—it is actively destructive. Behavioural research shows that the more frequently people check their investments, the more likely they are to make reactive decisions, often at the wrong times. Ironically, the very act of monitoring risk too closely increases the likelihood of experiencing it.

One of the reasons time reduces risk is compounding. Albert Einstein allegedly called compound interest the "eighth wonder of the world," and for good reason. It is not intuitive, but it is immensely powerful. A modest annual return, repeated consistently over time, grows geometrically. But the critical ingredient is time. Remove time from the equation, and compounding is just a theoretical curiosity. Let time do its work, and it becomes a force multiplier. *In investing, patience is not passive—it's the most active ingredient in long-term success.*

Time also introduces a behavioural advantage. When you align your investment decisions with a multi-decade horizon, you give yourself permission to detach from the noise. You stop asking, "Is this fund beating the market this quarter?" and start asking, "Will this strategy help me retire comfortably in twenty years?" That shift in time-frame reframes the entire psychological experience of investing. Anxiety gives way to perspective. Short-term losses become opportunities. Investing becomes a process, not a performance.

This is where SIPs—Systematic Investment Plans—come into their own. By automating investment over time, SIPs harness both dollar-cost averaging and time diversification. When you invest the same amount regularly, you buy more units when prices are low and fewer when they're high. Over time, this smooths out the effects of volatility. But perhaps more importantly, it builds discipline. It decouples your behaviour from market emotion and recouples it to a long-term habit. *SIPs are not just financial tools—they are behavioural frameworks rooted in the logic of time.*

Let's also consider inflation. Many investors forget that money loses value over time. If you keep £100,000 in cash for ten years with 3% annual inflation, it loses nearly a quarter of its purchasing power. Doing nothing is not risk-free—it's *guaranteed erosion.* Investing, despite its short-term bumps, offers a way to stay ahead of this silent predator. Over time, equities—though volatile—have historically outpaced inflation by a wide margin. Bonds and real estate, when used thoughtfully, also contribute to preserving and growing purchasing power. But again, the key is time. Without a long enough horizon, these assets can underperform, underwhelm, and unnerve. *But with time, they work.*

Sceptics might point to the Japanese stock market, which stagnated for decades after its 1989 peak. And they're right to raise it—it's a reminder that long-term success isn't guaranteed by time alone. Valuation at entry matters. Economic context matters. Diversification matters. No one should invest with blind faith. But even in Japan, investors who diversified globally, rebalanced regularly, and reinvested dividends fared significantly better than those who stayed local and static. Time reduces risk, but it does not absolve us from strategy.

So how long is "long enough"? The answer depends on your goals. If you're investing for retirement and you're in your 30s or 40s, your time horizon is measured in decades. That gives you latitude to take on more equity risk and absorb volatility. If you're closer to retirement, time is shorter—but still sufficient to require a plan. Even then, retirees don't withdraw their entire portfolio at once. Their money continues to be invested across time, even during retirement. Which means *time continues to matter, even after the accumulation phase ends.*

One of the best things an advisor or educator can do for an investor is to help them visualise time differently. Instead of thinking about their money as a lump sum subject to market forces, they should see it as a series of decisions stretched over decades. Each contribution, each rebalancing, each moment of staying the course—these are time's tools, not merely calendar artefacts. When time becomes part of the investor's identity, risk itself changes shape. It becomes manageable. Bearable. Even necessary.

Ultimately, the most dangerous form of risk is not the volatility you can see on a graph—it's the impulse to interrupt time before it has done its work. Selling during a downturn, chasing short-term returns, switching funds based on headlines—these are decisions made when time is ignored. Investors must protect their timeline as fiercely as they protect their capital. Because capital without time is speculation. *But capital with time is a strategy.*

This is the paradox that every serious investor must embrace: the path to financial peace lies not in avoiding risk, but in understanding that risk shrinks when stretched over time. Time is not just a background variable—it is the asset class you cannot buy but must earn. And for those willing to wait, it offers something rare in financial markets: *predictability*. Not in price, but in principle. Not in short-term returns, but in long-term resilience.

Understanding time as the great risk reducer is more than academic. It is practical, empowering, and deeply human. Because it allows us to invest not with panic, but with purpose. Not because we know what markets will do next, but because we understand what they do eventually. Time doesn't make risk disappear. It simply puts it where it belongs—*in perspective.*

The Real Risk: Not Investing at All

If you ask the average individual why they haven't invested yet, the answer usually pivots around fear—fear of loss, fear of complexity, fear of poor timing. These concerns are valid, but they are also misplaced. The uncomfortable truth is this: *not investing at all is far riskier than investing imperfectly*. It is not market downturns, volatility, or bad luck that destroy long-term wealth. It is inertia. And the consequences of inertia are quiet, cumulative, and devastatingly predictable.

Let's begin with inflation. Unlike stock market declines, which are sharp, visible, and headline-grabbing, inflation is stealthy. It erodes purchasing power gradually, invisibly. £100 today buys less than it did ten years ago—and dramatically less than it did twenty years ago. In the United Kingdom, the average annual inflation rate has hovered around 2–3% for decades. At just 2.5% inflation, the value of your money halves in approximately 28 years. This is not speculation. This is arithmetic. *If your money isn't growing, it's shrinking.* Every year you leave capital uninvested is a year it quietly loses value.

Now consider opportunity cost—the value of the returns you miss while waiting for the "right time." Suppose you delayed investing £10,000 in a simple equity index fund that averaged 8% annual growth. After ten years, you'd miss out on more than £11,000 in potential gains. And yet the delay often feels justified in the moment: "I'll invest once the market stabilises," or "I'll wait for the next dip."

But markets rarely offer perfect entry points. They are volatile by nature. Waiting for clarity is like waiting for the sky to stop being weather—it misunderstands the system itself.

The behavioural trap is clear: we overestimate the risk of action and underestimate the cost of inaction. This asymmetry is reinforced by psychology. When you lose money after investing, the pain is immediate and visceral. When you lose money by not investing, there's no visible loss—just the slow erosion of purchasing power and missed compounding. *But the impact is real, measurable, and permanent.*

There's also a deeper, more philosophical risk to never investing: dependence. Without capital growth, people remain tethered to labour. They must continue working indefinitely, not out of purpose, but necessity. Investing, done responsibly, is not about chasing returns—it's about buying freedom. Freedom from financial anxiety. Freedom to take risks in your career. Freedom to retire with dignity. Declining to invest is not a neutral choice. It is a choice to trade away those freedoms, knowingly or not.

Consider the impact of procrastination through the lens of compounding. If a 25-year-old invests £200 per month until age 65 at an average return of 8%, they accumulate roughly £700,000. If they wait until age 35 to begin, their ending value drops to around £300,000—even though they've only skipped ten years. That ten-year delay cuts their final outcome by more than half. *Time is not linear in investing—it's exponential.* Every year of hesitation costs more than the last.

And yet procrastination persists. Why? Because most people conflate comfort with safety. Keeping money in a savings account feels safe. It's visible. It doesn't fluctuate. But real safety is about outcomes, not feelings. A stable number on a bank statement is not safe if that number loses purchasing power year after year. Emotional safety often comes at the expense of financial reality.

Fear is another major culprit. Many non-investors imagine investing as a high-stakes casino—charts flying, fortunes rising and crashing. But investing, particularly in diversified funds and long-term strategies, is nothing like gambling. It's structured, probabilistic, and backed by real-world productivity. Companies generate profits, pay dividends, grow over time. Investing in these companies through funds is not speculation—it's *participation.* Participation in human progress, innovation, and enterprise.

Still, fear is potent. Memories of the 2008 financial crisis or the 2020 pandemic crash loom large. But fear is rarely contextualised properly. For example, during the COVID-19 panic, global markets dropped nearly 30% in a matter of weeks. But within months, they began recovering—and within a year, many indices hit all-time highs. Investors who panicked and pulled out locked in losses. Those who stayed put—or kept investing—benefited from the rebound. *Fear punishes reactivity. Time rewards patience.*

There is also a category of risk that's rarely discussed: the risk of regret. Imagine reaching retirement age and realising you've outlived your savings—not because you were reckless, but because you were overly cautious. This is not a hypothetical scenario. It's a growing reality for many who kept their money in low-yield vehicles or avoided markets altogether. The emotional toll of that regret—of having been "safe" for decades only to end up financially exposed—is profound. It is the hidden cost of not investing.

Importantly, the antidote to these risks is not blind optimism or reckless investing. It's intentionality. Start with small, regular investments. Use tools like SIPs to automate the process. Choose low-cost index funds to remove complexity and reduce risk. Focus on time in the market, not timing the market. And most of all, redefine what risk actually means. *Risk is not about temporary dips. It's about permanent disadvantages.*

Even the world's most respected financial thinkers agree. Nobel laureate economist Paul Samuelson once said, "Investing should be more like watching paint dry or watching grass grow. If you want excitement, take $800 and go to Las Vegas." The point is not to avoid all risk, but to take the right kind of risk—the kind that grows your money over time and helps you achieve real-world goals.

It's also worth recognising that financial systems are evolving in ways that make disciplined investing easier. Tools like robo-advisors, SIPs, and target-date funds have lowered the barriers to entry and reduced decision fatigue. You don't need to pick individual stocks or time the market. You need only to participate—early, consistently, and patiently. The question is no longer whether investing is accessible, but whether you're willing to embrace the responsibility of action.

And this, finally, brings us to the most personal form of risk: the risk to your own narrative. Every financial choice tells a story—not just about your money, but about your mindset. Choosing not to invest is often rooted in a story of avoidance, hesitation, or scarcity. But reframing that narrative—viewing investing as an act of stewardship, of future-building, of respect for your own potential—changes the energy entirely. *The first investment you make is in your identity as an investor.*

So while volatility makes headlines, and market downturns get televised, the real risk lives in the quiet corners—unread bank statements, delayed decisions, anxious what-ifs. The tragedy isn't that some investors lose money. It's that far more people never give themselves the chance to grow it. They wait. They worry. They opt out.

And in doing so, they accept the greatest risk of all: *the risk of doing nothing.*

Creating Your Own Comfort Zone of Risk

Risk in investing is not a universal concept—it's profoundly personal. Two individuals can react to the same portfolio drawdown in entirely opposite ways: one shrugs it off as a temporary fluctuation; the other experiences sleepless nights and second-guesses. The distinction lies not in their wealth, age, or intelligence, but in something subtler: *risk identity.* Yet too often, people invest based on generic advice or peer imitation, without any understanding of what level of volatility they can psychologically and emotionally endure. This subchapter aims to change that.

The financial industry has long attempted to standardise risk profiling, but most "risk tolerance" questionnaires are superficial and miss the essence of the issue. They focus on hypotheticals divorced from lived experience. A more useful tool is what we might call a *risk identity quiz*—not a survey that produces a score, but a reflective framework that helps investors understand the interplay between their temperament, life context, and financial aspirations. Because at the heart of successful investing is this simple but essential truth: *you need to find a strategy you can live with, not just one that looks good on paper.*

To illustrate the concept, consider two archetypal investors. Emma is 38, a public health researcher with a stable income, modest lifestyle, and low desire for dramatic financial outcomes. She values peace of mind over performance. Then there's Aarav, 35, an entrepreneur with variable income, a higher risk appetite, and an aggressive wealth-building goal. Both are intelligent, disciplined professionals. Yet if they were given identical portfolios, their experiences would diverge sharply. Emma might panic during a 20% correction; Aarav might see it as a buying opportunity. *The lesson is not about who's "better" at investing, but who's aligned.*

This alignment begins with recognising that your tolerance for risk is dynamic. It is not a static personality trait. It evolves with age, with life events, with changing responsibilities. The arrival of a child, the death of a parent, a business setback, or even just a bout of economic pessimism—all can shift your appetite for uncertainty. And that's not weakness. That's being human. *The goal isn't to suppress your emotions, but to integrate them intelligently into your decision-making.*

One of the clearest signals that an investor is misaligned with their risk identity is frequent tinkering—selling after dips, chasing top-performing funds, or constantly "rebalancing" in ways that feel more like emotional reactions than strategic adjustments. This kind of behaviour isn't just inefficient. It's expensive. Studies consistently show that the average investor underperforms the very funds they invest in, simply because they enter and exit at the wrong times. And often, this dysfunction stems not from poor intellect but from poor fit.

So how does one go about constructing a comfort zone of risk?

Start with *cash flow realism.* Before you think about fund type or portfolio construction, understand what you can consistently invest without strain. If your monthly SIP amount forces you into short-term liquidity issues, you're setting yourself up for tension and, eventually, abandonment. Your investment rhythm must align with your financial breathing rate. If that's £150 a month, fine. If it's £1,500, also fine. *Sustainability is more powerful than size.*

Next, assess your *emotional bandwidth.* Ask yourself honestly: How would you feel if your portfolio dropped 10% in a month? Would you feel compelled to check it daily? Would it dominate your dinner table conversations? Or would you trust the process and carry on with life? Your answer to this thought experiment isn't about being brave or disciplined. It's about being honest. If the mere idea of a 10% drop induces anxiety, you likely need a more conservative asset allocation. Not forever—but for now. Over time, as you build exposure and experience, your tolerance may grow organically.

Now layer in *time horizon.* The longer you can leave your investments untouched, the more risk you can afford to take—mathematically and psychologically. Historical data shows that equity market returns become increasingly predictable over longer periods. A one-year holding may be a coin toss. A ten-year holding smooths the curve dramatically. But this statistical reassurance only matters if you can actually let the money sit. If you know you might need access to it within three years—for a house deposit, education, or starting a business—then your comfort zone narrows. *Risk identity is part temperament, part timeline.*

Then comes *fund selection.* Once your psychological and temporal parameters are clear, you can begin to choose funds that mirror your comfort zone. Someone with low volatility tolerance might opt for a mix of conservative hybrid funds and short-duration bond funds, supplemented by a small equity allocation. Another person might favour aggressive equity funds with occasional thematic exposure. The point is not to chase returns, but to *construct a portfolio you won't abandon when things get bumpy.* Because the best portfolio is not the one with the highest backtested CAGR. It's the one you actually stick with.

And here's where the identity piece becomes transformative. When you craft a strategy that reflects your inner world—not just external advice—you begin to *trust yourself*. You become immune to FOMO. You stop comparing your returns to friends or internet influencers. You stop reacting to headlines. Your portfolio becomes a quiet extension of your values and vision, not a source of daily drama.

Real-world stories illustrate this principle far better than theory. Consider Nina, a 42-year-old architect who had never invested before and was paralysed by the thought of losing money. Her financial planner started her with a 70% debt and 30% equity hybrid fund, paired with a SIP of just £100 per month. Within six months, Nina had not only stopped checking her portfolio obsessively but had increased her SIP voluntarily. She felt empowered—not because the markets were booming, but because she had redefined risk in terms she could emotionally digest.

Contrast that with Dev, a 29-year-old software engineer who jumped into sectoral funds after seeing a friend's one-year returns. When tech stocks corrected, his portfolio dropped 25%—and he sold everything in a panic. It wasn't his knowledge that failed him. It was a misalignment between ambition and resilience. Dev wasn't "wrong" for trying something bold. He was simply mismatched. If he had started with a broader, diversified equity fund and gradually built confidence, the story might have ended very differently.

The key takeaway is this: *you don't need to be fearless—you need to be fitted.* Your risk identity is not about being conservative or aggressive. It's about knowing what level of uncertainty your mind, heart, and life can tolerate—today. That identity can be revisited. It can evolve. But it must be named.

If you're unsure where to start, consider asking yourself a few anchoring questions:

When I see red numbers in my portfolio, what's my instinctive reaction?

What's the longest period I could confidently leave my investments untouched?

How much monthly investment can I make without feeling constrained?

Am I investing to maximise returns, or to build a sustainable future?

Do I want to participate in markets or outperform them—and am I equipped for that?

These questions don't give you a score. They give you a shape. A silhouette of your comfort zone. From there, everything else—funds, allocations, timeframes—can follow.

Ultimately, the purpose of investing isn't to impress anyone. It's not to win games, beat benchmarks, or "time" anything. It's to create a financial architecture that supports the kind of life you want to live—with as little stress, regret, or confusion as possible. And that architecture must begin with the foundation of *personal alignment.* Once you know your risk identity, you can build a strategy that feels not just acceptable, but *peaceful.*

That's not a soft benefit. That's the cornerstone of discipline. And discipline, more than any market condition, is what determines long-term success.

Chapter 8
Choosing Your Fund, Choosing Your Future

Rewrite the following article to pass AI-detection tools while retaining its professional, intellectually engaging, and authoritative tone.

Rephrase and restructure the content to feel human-authored, with a writing style that reflects the subtle imperfections and expressive flow of a skilled writer.

Specifically: – Vary sentence structures, paragraph rhythms, and transition choices to avoid algorithmic patterns

– Introduce occasional conversational touches or rhetorical asides where appropriate

– Make subtle word choices or phrase shifts that sound natural but aren't statistically predictable

– Avoid "perfectly smooth" sentence-to-sentence transitions—a little friction is more human

– Maintain the original meaning, flow, facts, and paragraphing

– Do not simplify or summarise—this is not a paraphrasing task, but a creative re-authorship

– Use British English conventions

– Ensure the result still reads like it was written by a seasoned nonfiction writer with intellectual and emotional depth

Output only the reworked article text. No explanations. No headers. No setup language.

Every investment decision is, at its core, a life decision wearing financial clothes. When someone selects a mutual fund, they aren't just picking a blend of stocks and bonds—they're expressing a hope, a timeline, and a personal definition of security. The act of fund selection is often framed as a data-driven, analytical process. But beneath the spreadsheets and performance charts lies something far more human: the desire for a future that feels both possible and peaceful. To choose a fund wisely, we must first understand what we're really choosing it for.

This chapter begins with a foundational principle: clarity before complexity. The biggest mistake investors make is not selecting the wrong fund, but not knowing why they're investing at all. Ask most people why they're putting money into mutual funds, and the answers are vague—"for the long term," "to grow wealth," or "just to be safe." These are aspirations, not goals. They lack the emotional specificity required to make intelligent investment decisions. It's the difference between saying "I want to be healthy" and saying "I want to be able to hike with my grandchildren at age 70 without pain." One is abstract. The other drives action.

Good investing begins not with the market, but with the self. Are you investing for early retirement, or for your child's education? Are you building a legacy for your family, or simply seeking peace of mind after years of financial stress? Your answer need not be sophisticated. But it must be honest. Because the clarity of your intention will shape the design of your portfolio far more effectively than any macroeconomic forecast or fund ranking ever could.

Once this clarity is established, the technical task of choosing the right fund becomes significantly more grounded. Different goals have different time horizons, risk tolerances, and liquidity needs—and thus, different optimal fund types. A short-term goal like a house deposit might call for a low-volatility, debt-oriented fund. A mid-term goal, such as a sabbatical or child's high school tuition, might be best served by a balanced or hybrid fund. A long-term goal like retirement or intergenerational wealth-building opens the door to high-equity allocations and thematic exposure. This is goal-based investing—not as jargon, but as practical alignment.

And yet, even with goal clarity, many investors falter at the next stage: interpreting the fund fact sheet. This document, intended to inform, often intimidates. It's filled with ratios, sector allocations, historical returns, benchmark comparisons. But at its best, a fund fact sheet is not a data dump—it's a narrative. It tells you what the fund believes in, how it behaves in different market climates, and whether its strategy aligns with your needs. Reading a fund fact sheet should feel less like reading a menu of ingredients and more like understanding a chef's philosophy. Are they chasing trends? Do they stick to fundamentals? Are they consistent in style or opportunistic? Behind every number lies a story. You just have to be taught how to read it.

The real art, then, lies in bridging emotional clarity with technical comprehension. Most people are taught that good investing means suppressing emotion and focusing solely on logic. That's a half-truth. Emotionless investing is impossible—and undesirable. What matters is not removing emotion, but reconciling it with rationality. You can honour your fear of volatility while still choosing a smart asset allocation. You can acknowledge your desire for stability while building in growth potential. Investing is not a war between heart and mind. It is a negotiation.

Yet even after aligning goals and interpreting data, many investors still feel paralysed. Faced with dozens—sometimes hundreds—of fund options, decision fatigue sets in. Research becomes a trap, not a tool. Hours are spent comparing marginal differences in 3-year returns or trying to forecast fund manager turnover. This paralysis by analysis is not a sign of laziness—it's the inevitable result of a system that treats fund selection as an IQ test rather than a values-based process.

To break through this fog, this chapter introduces minimalist frameworks for decision-making—tools that cut through noise and anchor the process in simplicity. These tools don't aim to guarantee the perfect fund, but to narrow the field to the right fit. Because success in mutual fund investing doesn't come from picking the "best" fund in hindsight. It comes from picking a good fund that you can stick with in real time.

And sticking with a fund isn't just about returns. It's about trust. Trust in your goals. Trust in your process. Trust in the alignment between your chosen fund and your chosen future. When that trust exists, you check your portfolio less. You worry less. You resist distractions. You stop asking whether you're doing what everyone else is doing and start asking whether you're doing what you need.

This chapter will not overwhelm you with jargon or drown you in performance tables. Instead, it will equip you with a practical, emotionally intelligent framework for fund selection—rooted in your goals, refined by your understanding, and sustained by your discipline. It will walk you through how to think, not just what to think. It will make fund selection feel less like a guessing game and more like a conversation—with yourself, your future, and your values.

To choose a fund well is to take control of your financial story. It is to say: I am not outsourcing my future to chance or to noise. I am designing it, consciously. Not perfectly—but thoughtfully. And that thoughtfulness, compounded over time, is what builds wealth that is not just financial, but felt.

Because ultimately, the fund you choose is not just a vehicle. It's a statement. About who you are, what you value, and what kind of future you're building towards. Choose well—and you don't just choose a product. You choose a path.

Clarity First: What Are You Investing For?

Most people begin their investment journey by asking *what* to buy. Which mutual fund? Which stock? Which asset class? The unspoken assumption is that financial success begins with market knowledge—facts, ratios, returns, rankings. But seasoned investors understand a deeper truth: *strategy begins not with selection, but with self-awareness.* The real starting point is not choosing between equity or debt, active or passive. It's asking, with unflinching honesty: *what am I actually investing for?* That question, properly understood, is not logistical—it's emotional.

We have been conditioned to approach goal-setting as an exercise in calculation. Set a target number. Back-calculate based on inflation and expected return. Allocate monthly savings accordingly. While this is technically sound, it is psychologically barren. A spreadsheet does not inspire commitment. A projection does not withstand panic. In contrast, *emotional clarity*—understanding what freedom, stability, or legacy mean to *you*—anchors discipline far more than any formula. People don't stay invested because a CAGR tells them to. They stay invested because they can see, vividly, the life they are building toward.

Consider the difference between two investors. One says, "I want to retire with ₹3 crores." The other says, "I want to be free of working by 55 so I can care for my ageing parents without financial pressure." Both might require the same amount, but the second investor has a narrative, not just a number. That narrative becomes a filter through which market noise loses power. When markets wobble, the first investor may second-guess the entire plan. The second can visualise their parents' peace, and that image keeps them grounded.

This is not soft thinking—it is rigorous introspection. Clarity of purpose is what transforms vague saving into strategic investing. And it demands a higher standard than generic goals like "retirement" or "wealth creation." Those are categories, not convictions. What does retirement actually look like to you? Is it passive income or active reinvention? Do you imagine travel, teaching, gardening, or simply not worrying about bills? The specificity of your future vision determines how you'll emotionally respond to the volatility and patience required to fund it.

Investment, then, becomes a tool for identity design. Each rupee allocated is a vote—not just for financial return, but for a version of your future self. That may sound philosophical, but its practical implications are immense. A person investing for peace of mind in five years should not hold the same portfolio as someone investing for their child's inheritance thirty years hence. The timelines, tolerances, and fund structures differ—*but those differences only become clear after the deeper emotional audit.*

Many investors make the mistake of reverse-engineering their goals to match what they think the market will reward. They see what funds are performing, what others are buying, and retrofit their goals accordingly. This is a recipe for short-termism and anxiety. The better approach is to begin *inside-out*: define what matters to you, then seek financial tools that align with those values and time horizons. The clarity must precede the complexity.

This kind of introspective goal-setting also reduces the psychological risk of regret. It's not uncommon for high earners in their 40s and 50s to report a nagging discontent with their portfolios—not because the numbers are poor, but because they can't trace the money to anything meaningful. They invested, often diligently, but in a way that felt abstract and disconnected. Without emotional anchoring, even successful investments can feel hollow. The goal isn't just returns; it's resonance.

Let's also be honest: not every goal will feel noble. Some people invest for revenge success—to prove something to a parent, a peer group, or an internal critic. Others invest because they fear being a burden or losing relevance. These motivations may not sound aspirational, but they are real. They deserve recognition. Emotional clarity is not about sanitising your reasons. It's about surfacing them so you can align them consciously. Investing is not therapy, but it does demand honesty with yourself.

Moreover, your goals will evolve. A twenty-eight-year-old investing for early retirement might find, at thirty-five, that their focus shifts to their child's education or to launching a business. That's not a failure of planning—it's a feature of being human. Emotional clarity is not static. It's iterative. What matters is not having one perfectly fixed goal, but being willing to reassess your investment map as your internal compass shifts.

Goal clarity also simplifies decision-making. When you know *why* you're investing, it becomes easier to say no to distractions. Hot stock tips, trending funds, and fear-based headlines lose their power. If your goal is to create a stable income stream by 2035, then you can immediately filter out products and strategies that don't serve that end. You are not resisting temptation through willpower. You are filtering through design. That's a much more sustainable approach.

This process of emotional goal-setting does not require a financial adviser—though a good one can help ask the right questions. It requires solitude, honesty, and perhaps a pen and paper more than a spreadsheet. Ask yourself:

– What life experiences do I want to protect or enable?
– What emotional state am I seeking—freedom, security, status, peace?
– When will I need the money—and for what, precisely?
– What kind of financial stress can I tolerate—and what kind can I not?

These are not mechanical questions. They are formative ones. They reorient investing from being a game of returns to being a practice of alignment. Without that alignment, even a "winning" portfolio can lead to misgivings. With it, even a modest portfolio becomes meaningful.

Importantly, this approach shifts the tone of investing from performance anxiety to purpose-driven action. The goal is not to beat benchmarks or outsmart the market. It is to fund a life you find valuable. That may sound less thrilling than speculative trading or financial engineering, but it is far more enduring. *Clarity scales. Complexity fatigues.*

As you continue through this chapter and this book, every framework, fund analysis, and decision tool must be tethered to this central anchor: what are you investing for? Not as a performance objective. As a life intention. That single piece of clarity will do more to protect your confidence during downturns and distractions than any technical metric.

To build wealth with integrity is to honour both your numbers and your narrative. Without the latter, the former can become hollow. So before asking *what to invest in*, ask yourself—*what am I building? Who is it for? And what will it feel like to get there?*

Your answer is your strategy. Everything else is execution.

Matching Goals to Fund Types

The most elegant investment portfolios are not those chasing the highest returns—they're those precisely aligned with the investor's real-life objectives. The trouble is, most people don't build portfolios. They assemble them. Bit by bit, over time, through a patchwork of tips, past performance, and hearsay, people end up holding a mix of funds that were never designed to coexist. And because the starting point is often the product and not the purpose, they find themselves reacting to markets instead of progressing toward meaningful goals. Goal-based investing is not a buzzword—it's the foundation of coherence in personal finance. The key is not to invest broadly. It's to invest deliberately.

But what does it mean, in practice, to match goals to fund types? It begins with time. Time is not merely a passive variable in investment—it is the organising principle. Every financial goal lives on a timeline, and the nature of that timeline should dictate the risk you're willing to take, the type of fund you choose, and the behaviour you commit to. *Time doesn't just influence returns; it calibrates expectations.* And yet most investors skip this thinking entirely, jumping from desire to action without pausing to classify their goals.

Let's define the distinctions with clarity. A **short-term goal** is one that demands liquidity within the next 1 to 3 years. Think of a wedding, a down payment, or an emergency buffer. These are non-negotiable timelines—markets don't get a say in whether the money is needed. In such cases, safety and accessibility matter more than growth. Equity exposure here is reckless. For these goals, low-duration debt funds, liquid funds, or ultra-short-term funds offer a more stable path. The key is capital preservation, not yield maximisation.

A **mid-term goal** spans the 3 to 7-year range. It might involve planning for a child's primary education, a sabbatical, or relocating cities. The timeline here is firm but not immediate. This opens a window for modest equity exposure—perhaps 20% to 40%—via hybrid funds or conservative balanced funds. The aim is to balance some capital appreciation with a cushion of stability. For many investors, these are the most mismanaged goals: too long for pure debt, too short for pure equity, and often neglected in favour of binary asset choices. The real answer lies in nuance.

A **long-term goal** typically stretches beyond 7 years—retirement, wealth creation, intergenerational transfer. These are the goals that compound time with strategy. Here, equity becomes not just acceptable but essential. The volatility of stocks is transformed by the length of the horizon—what looks like risk on a one-year chart looks like resilience over a decade. Equity-oriented mutual funds—whether diversified large-cap, mid-cap, or index-based—can form the core of long-term portfolios. The primary threat in this category is not market fluctuation but investor impatience.

Now here's where it becomes interesting. *The same fund can be perfect for one investor and dangerous for another—solely depending on the timeline of use.* A small-cap fund may be an excellent choice for a 30-year-old investing for retirement but wholly inappropriate for someone needing access to funds in three years. This isn't a reflection of the fund's quality—it's a matter of fit. The real art of fund selection lies in matching *tempo to temperament.*

This mapping exercise also requires emotional honesty. People often conflate the timeline they *wish* they had with the one they *actually* have. Someone saving for a home down payment in 24 months might tell themselves they can "stretch it" to four years to justify taking on riskier funds. But markets don't negotiate. If the equity fund dips at the wrong time, the plan collapses. The role of the investor is not to bend reality to market forecasts. It's to choose instruments that respect the truth of their timelines.

Let's also address the myth of one-size-fits-all funds. Many investors seek the "best" mutual fund—one that can serve all purposes. This is a flawed pursuit. Your financial life contains multitudes. You might be saving simultaneously for a holiday next year, your child's college in ten years, and retirement in thirty. These are not variations of a single goal. They are separate projects, and they deserve separate vehicles. A single-fund strategy cannot cater to this complexity. The minimalist portfolio is not the one with the fewest funds. It's the one with the clearest fund-purpose link.

This is why goal-matching also solves the problem of emotional mismanagement. When investors panic-sell equity funds during a market dip, it is rarely because of market ignorance—it is because they were using the wrong fund for the wrong goal. If a person has parked their emergency fund in a volatile equity fund, any downturn feels like a crisis. The problem wasn't the market—it was the mismatch. By clarifying purpose, you reduce panic.

That clarity also sharpens accountability. When your fund is explicitly tied to your child's university fees ten years out, you're more likely to track it with intention. The abstraction disappears. Your portfolio becomes a visualisation of your future responsibilities. Investing no longer feels like a random act of discipline. It becomes an extension of your values.

Some fund houses now offer goal-based solutions—target maturity funds for fixed outcomes, goal-labelled SIPs, and even digital platforms that link fund buckets to goal icons. These tools are useful, but the responsibility still lies with the investor to map the correct instrument to the correct goal. Automation does not replace awareness. The true task is not just to assign a fund—it is to understand *why that fund belongs where it does.*

A useful mental model is to imagine your financial life as a shelf with three compartments: urgent, upcoming, and unfolding. The urgent shelf needs stability. The upcoming shelf needs balance. The unfolding shelf needs growth. Place your funds accordingly. If a fund feels hard to categorise, it likely doesn't belong—or your goal lacks definition.

And don't mistake past returns as justification. Just because a fund has performed well historically does not mean it aligns with your current objectives. Past performance is not a goal—it is a statistic. The better question is not "how well has this fund done?" but "how well can this fund serve *my* goal, given *my* timeline and tolerance?"

When fund matching is done well, it produces an unexpected benefit: peace of mind. Not because markets become less volatile, but because your financial decisions become less reactive. You know which part of your portfolio is responsible for what, and you don't expect every rupee to do every job. That kind of clarity is liberating.

The goal, ultimately, is not just technical precision. It's emotional coherence. Investing should feel aligned—not just in returns, but in meaning. Matching goals to fund types isn't about optimising for return alone. It's about building a structure where each financial action contributes, specifically and visibly, to a life that makes sense to *you*. That is the architecture of confidence. Everything else is decoration.

Reading a Fund Fact Sheet Like a Story

Most people approach a fund fact sheet as though it were a piece of technical machinery—something to be decoded by number-crunchers or financial analysts. It's no surprise then that the average investor skims it for star ratings or recent performance and leaves the rest unread. Yet hidden in plain sight, beneath the percentages and tables, lies the narrative heartbeat of the fund. When read with care and context, a fund fact sheet doesn't just tell you what a fund has done. It tells you who it is, what it believes, and whether it belongs in your life. The goal isn't just to extract data. It's to recognise alignment.

At its core, a fund fact sheet is not a neutral document. It is a curated portrait—a fund's attempt to explain itself to the investing public. Every number, every chart, every sentence is making a claim, and reading it effectively means going beyond surface interpretation to understand what those claims mean in practice. Like any good story, a fact sheet has a protagonist (the fund manager), a setting (the market and macro context), a plot (investment strategy), and a history (performance trajectory). The key is to connect these elements to the reader's own goals, values, and risk boundaries.

Let's begin with the **fund objective**—typically the first section on any fact sheet. This is where the fund sets out its mission statement.

But most investors gloss over it. Why? Because it often sounds vague: "The scheme seeks to generate long-term capital appreciation…" Nearly every equity fund says something similar. But a closer read reveals subtle distinctions. One fund might prioritise growth through large-cap stocks; another may seek value in under-researched mid-cap opportunities. The difference is not just linguistic. It reflects a fundamental difference in investment worldview. *Your task is not just to note the objective—it is to ask whether that philosophy fits your intended purpose.*

Next comes **asset allocation**. This is where many readers' eyes glaze over. But this section reveals the fund's true risk posture. An "equity-oriented hybrid fund" with a 75% allocation to equities behaves very differently from one with a 60% tilt. The presence of arbitrage strategies, duration bets in debt components, or international exposure—all these shape the fund's behaviour under stress. Look for signals of *how the fund earns returns, not just where it deploys capital.* This is how you distinguish between a fund that is stable by design and one that is merely lucky in timing.

The **fund manager's profile** often feels like a formality, but it is far from irrelevant. The manager is the human hand behind the numbers. Their experience, track record across market cycles, and tenure with the fund all speak to stability and style consistency. A manager with a strong contrarian streak may underperform in bull markets and shine during volatility. Another may ride momentum trends skillfully but falter in sideways markets. *Knowing who is steering the ship helps you anticipate how it might behave when the tide turns.*

The **portfolio composition** is the fund's most revealing chapter—its cast of characters, so to speak. The top 10 holdings are often published, but the real story is in the sectors, themes, and position sizes. A fund claiming to be diversified but with 40% in financial services is effectively making a macro bet. If the portfolio is heavily skewed toward cyclicals, it will likely be more volatile. If it leans on defensives, expect steadier returns but less upside in rallies. Also observe how concentrated the portfolio is: does it hold 25 stocks or 75? A concentrated portfolio signals high conviction, but also higher idiosyncratic risk. *The spread of holdings tells you how the manager handles uncertainty.*

Now to the **performance table**—where most people rush first. But raw returns, devoid of context, tell you very little. A 15% annual return looks impressive until you realise the benchmark returned 17%. A 5% return may look modest, but if achieved with half the volatility of the market, it's commendable. Look at *rolling returns* rather than calendar year returns—they show how the fund performs across multiple overlapping periods, not just during lucky or unlucky windows. Pay attention to *downside capture ratios*—how much the fund tends to lose when markets fall. *A fund that wins less but loses far less is often more powerful over the long term than a flashy performer with deep drawdowns.*

Expense ratio is often treated as a footnote, but it deserves front-row attention. Two funds with identical portfolios and philosophies may deliver dramatically different outcomes over time if one charges 0.75% and the other 2.25%. Expenses compound just like returns—but in reverse. If you're investing for 15 years, even a small difference in costs can translate into lakhs of rupees. Importantly, a high expense ratio does not always mean bad value. *What matters is what you're getting in return for the cost.* If the fund's research depth, strategy uniqueness, and manager skill deliver genuine alpha, a higher fee may be justified. But blind premium should never be paid.

The **risk metrics**—standard deviation, Sharpe ratio, beta—can sound intimidating but need not be. You don't need a finance degree to interpret them meaningfully. Standard deviation gives a sense of how much the fund's returns vary from its average—essentially, how jumpy it is. Sharpe ratio adjusts returns for that volatility—higher is better. Beta tells you how much the fund tends to move relative to the market. A beta of 1 means it moves in lockstep; above 1 means it amplifies market moves; below 1 means it tempers them. *These numbers help you match the fund's behavioural DNA to your own emotional risk profile.*

Perhaps the most underrated section of a fact sheet is the **commentary**—where the fund house provides a narrative perspective. This is where you hear the fund's voice directly. How does it interpret recent performance? What themes is it favouring? How does it view upcoming risks? Some managers communicate with refreshing honesty, acknowledging missteps and detailing forward-looking adjustments. Others offer vague platitudes. The style of communication tells you a lot about the culture of the fund house. *Trust is built not just through numbers but through transparent thought.*

When you read a fund fact sheet like a story, you begin to notice patterns. You stop asking, "What has this fund done?" and start asking, "What kind of character is this fund?" Is it patient or opportunistic? Is it steady or bold? Does it chase trends or build deep conviction? And, crucially, does it complement the rest of your portfolio—or duplicate it? Just as a good novel builds a cast of complementary roles, so too should your fund selections.

Reading fund literature this way also protects you from hype. You are no longer swayed by a single year of strong performance or an advertisement highlighting a trophy. Instead, you assess whether the fund's strategy is repeatable, whether the team behind it is stable, and whether the philosophy matches your purpose. *This is the difference between reacting to noise and responding to narrative.*

A fact sheet, when read properly, becomes a portal of alignment. It moves from being a data sheet to a mirror—reflecting whether your investment truly fits your goals, values, and temperament. Numbers matter, yes. But the story behind those numbers matters more. Every fund is a belief system wrapped in a portfolio. Learn to read it as such, and you stop selecting funds randomly. You start selecting them meaningfully. That is how an investor moves from confusion to conviction. Not through guesswork, but through literacy.

Decision Fatigue and How to Escape It

Most investors don't fail because they lack intelligence. They fail because they lack clarity at the moment of choice. In theory, the more data we have, the better decisions we should make. But the psychology of decision-making tells a very different story. After a certain point, more choice leads to *less* action, not more. And when that choice is emotionally loaded—like where to put your savings for the next 20 years—the paralysis can become near-total. This isn't a failure of willpower. It's a predictable outcome of cognitive overload. Welcome to decision fatigue: the silent, invisible tax on modern investors.

Every time you compare two mutual funds, read a market commentary, or tweak your asset allocation spreadsheet, you make a mental withdrawal from a finite pool of decision energy. This pool is not inexhaustible. Studies in behavioural science have shown that we each have a limited capacity for high-quality decision-making on any given day. The more decisions you make—especially those requiring judgment and trade-offs—the faster that quality deteriorates. By evening, even accomplished professionals are more likely to choose what's easy over what's right. Investment decisions made in that state tend to favour the comfortable, the familiar, or the most recently seen.

This is where the fund industry inadvertently exacerbates the problem. Instead of helping people make better decisions, it bombards them with an ever-expanding array of choices. There are thousands of mutual funds available in every category: large-cap, mid-cap, flexi-cap, sectoral, thematic, ESG, value, momentum, multi-asset, and dozens more. Each comes with its own brochure, narrative, and back-tested performance. The result isn't empowerment. It's exhaustion. And exhausted investors don't optimise—they either delay or default.

Paralysis by analysis is not a sign of laziness or incompetence. It is a consequence of misplaced strategy. Many investors, especially conscientious ones, believe that more research guarantees better outcomes. They consume fund reviews, track NAV movements, attend webinars, and compare historical returns. But beyond a certain threshold, this approach begins to degrade judgment rather than improve it. The illusion of control replaces actual clarity. *You cannot research your way out of ambiguity.*

So how do we escape this trap without resorting to mindless automation or blind faith?

The first principle is *conscious constraint.* Not all decisions deserve equal attention. One of the most powerful things an investor can do is to narrow their range of acceptable choices *before* they enter the selection process. That means deciding, in advance, what kind of investor you are, what kinds of funds align with your goals, and what types of complexity you are unwilling to tolerate. For example, if you are investing for long-term wealth creation and prefer broad market exposure, eliminate sectoral and thematic funds from your universe entirely. You don't need to evaluate what you'll never consider.

Second, embrace *minimalist frameworks*. One of the most effective tools is the "Good Enough" checklist. Instead of looking for the perfect fund, ask if a fund meets five clear thresholds: Is the expense ratio reasonable? Is the fund house credible and consistent? Does the fund manager have at least three years of tenure? Is the performance consistent relative to peers, not just the index? Does the portfolio align with your risk profile? If all five check out, stop digging. Perfection is the enemy of implementation. *The right fund held with discipline is more powerful than the ideal fund held with anxiety.*

Another useful strategy is to apply the principle of *category-level clarity*. Don't compare every fund to every other fund. Compare only within categories. Large-cap funds should be evaluated against other large-cap funds. Hybrid funds against other hybrid funds. This reduces cross-category noise and prevents irrelevant data from hijacking your mental model. It also trains your intuition to recognise patterns within relevant cohorts. *Effective decisions come not from analysing everything but from analysing the right things repeatedly.*

Time-blocked decision-making is another underrated method. Allocate a fixed window once a quarter—say, the first Saturday of every third month—to review your investments. Outside that window, refuse to engage with performance tracking or fund comparisons. This rhythm not only preserves your cognitive energy but also immunises you against short-term market noise. When your mind knows that there is a designated space for action, it is less tempted to act impulsively in between. *Discipline is easier to enforce when it's tied to structure rather than emotion.*

Decision fatigue is also driven by a deep, often unspoken fear: the fear of getting it wrong. Many investors would rather defer than choose, because the act of choosing makes them responsible for the outcome. This is where reframing helps. Instead of asking, "What's the best fund for me?" ask, "What is a fund I can live with peacefully for the next five years?" The goal shifts from optimisation to alignment. You are not trying to pick a winner. You are trying to design a relationship with volatility, return, and risk that you can sustain without regret. *The best decision is not the one with the highest projected return—it's the one you won't abandon prematurely.*

There is also an emotional dimension. Investors often confuse research with reassurance. They keep analysing as a way to soothe anxiety. But the anxiety never truly goes away—because the research never ends. Recognising this trap is liberating. If your goal is emotional security, it is better met through structural safeguards—like SIPs, diversified allocation, and pre-committed holding periods—than through more data. *Information is not the antidote to insecurity. Conviction is.*

Minimalist investing doesn't mean careless investing. It means recognising the asymmetry between what matters and what merely appears to matter. Most fund fact sheets contain more data than the average investor needs. Most portfolio dashboards encourage over-monitoring. Most industry commentary is designed to provoke churn. Knowing what to ignore is as valuable as knowing what to examine. As the saying goes, *simplicity is not about less—it's about clarity.*

Consider the example of Karthik, a 35-year-old salaried professional with a young child and ageing parents. He used to spend hours each weekend comparing mutual fund options, switching between platforms, and debating allocation tweaks. Despite his best intentions, he felt increasingly unsure and dissatisfied. After a financial coaching session, he implemented three rules: only invest in two categories—flexi-cap and balanced advantage; only check performance once a quarter; and review the portfolio once a year unless something major changed. Within months, his confidence improved, and he stopped second-guessing every move. His portfolio didn't suddenly outperform—but *he* did. He stuck with his plan.

Or take Priya, a 29-year-old freelancer who had been paralysed by the idea of investing at all. Every time she began, she felt overwhelmed by jargon and choices. A mentor advised her to follow the "One Fund Rule": just start with one SIP in a large-cap index fund, automate it, and revisit the rest later. That was two years ago. She now has three funds, a growing corpus, and most importantly, a sense of peace. The point wasn't the sophistication of her portfolio—it was the clarity of her process. *Progress begins when perfection ceases to be the prerequisite.*

Ultimately, escaping decision fatigue is about regaining trust—not in the markets, but in your own ability to choose wisely and act consistently. That trust comes from filtering noise, embracing process over prediction, and recognising that not every variable deserves your time. Investing doesn't reward the person who knows the most. It rewards the person who can make a good decision and stand by it long enough for it to work. That's not a technical skill. It's a psychological edge.

So ask yourself: How can I reduce the number of decisions I need to make without reducing the quality of my outcomes? How can I replace mental churn with structural clarity? And above all, how can I create a system where the next step is always obvious, not because I've optimised every detail, but because I've simplified the choices that matter? When you begin to answer those questions, you'll find not only better investments, but a better investor staring back at you in the mirror.

Chapter 9
How to Actually Start Investing

Knowing what to do and actually doing it are two entirely different challenges. Many readers reach this point feeling intellectually persuaded, emotionally prepared, yet practically immobilised. The concepts make sense, the principles resonate, but the act of opening an account, setting up a SIP, or picking a fund can still feel clouded in mystery—or worse, hidden behind bureaucratic layers. That hesitation isn't laziness; it is uncertainty. Questions like "Which platform should I trust?" or "What if I choose wrongly?" are entirely reasonable. Left unresolved, they can postpone financial progress for years.

This chapter is designed to strip away that ambiguity. It doesn't assume prior expertise, nor does it condescend. Instead, it provides a detailed, approachable roadmap for transforming intention into action. Because at the end of the day, investing is practice, not theory. And practice starts with one crucial step: implementation.

The first step is choosing your entry point. In today's digital landscape, the options are extensive—online brokers, wealth-tech platforms, direct mutual fund portals, robo-advisors, mobile apps that integrate multiple services. Each presents a different balance of control, simplicity, and cost. Some platforms are tailored for beginners, offering guided fund selection and SIP recommendations. Others prioritise depth, with analytics dashboards, portfolio visualisation, and international fund access. There is no universal "best" platform—only the one that feels frictionless to you.

The process begins with Know Your Customer (KYC) verification. While it may sound bureaucratic, it is largely paperless today. Aadhaar-based e-KYC or brief video verification usually takes under fifteen minutes. Following that, you'll open a mutual fund folio or a demat account, depending on whether your investments are direct mutual funds or through an integrated broker. The key is to avoid platform-hopping. Select one, complete the setup, and start. Complexity at this stage often masks procrastination.

Next comes the act of starting. For most beginners, a monthly Systematic Investment Plan (SIP) in a well-diversified fund—often an index or flexi-cap fund—is the simplest route. But setting up a SIP is more than technical; it is a behavioural commitment. You decide to prioritise your future self before anyone else. Entering an amount, selecting a date, automating the debit—seemingly mundane actions—signal a profound transformation: from reactive saver to proactive investor.

Yet many hesitate here too. How much is enough? Will I be "locked in"? SIPs are flexible. You can pause, increase, decrease, or stop them entirely. The most important thing is to start somewhere. Even ₹1,000 a month communicates to your brain: you have begun. From consistency comes comfort; from comfort comes conviction.

The chapter then widens the lens: what if you wish to diversify beyond domestic markets? Global investing has become increasingly accessible. Indian investors can now reach US equities, global ETFs, and thematic international funds via feeder funds or direct foreign brokers. But mechanics are secondary; purpose is primary. Are you seeking to hedge currency risk, access innovation-driven sectors like AI and biotech, or dilute domestic volatility? Matching intent to investment ensures that international exposure enhances diversification rather than chasing novelty.

Once implementation begins, monitoring emerges as the next challenge. Too little attention leads to drift; too much invites emotional reactivity. Effective oversight strikes a balance. Monthly reflection—not daily reaction—is the goal. Set alerts for missed SIPs, use dashboards to review allocations, and schedule quarterly check-ins to assess alignment with goals, risk tolerance, and life context. Monitoring is not about controlling the market; it is about maintaining awareness without obsession.

Portfolios must also evolve as life changes. Promotions, new children, relocations, ageing parents—each shifts horizons, liquidity needs, and emotional capacity. Rebalancing is not about chasing returns or timing markets; it is personal realignment. This chapter guides you on when and how to rebalance, and why, so your portfolio mirrors your life, not the market's mood swings.

Consider Arjun, a 28-year-old software engineer in Bangalore. After six months of research, he was paralysed by choice, endlessly tweaking spreadsheets without starting. A mentor advised: select any broad-market fund, set up a ₹2,000 SIP, and review in thirty days. That single step broke inertia. Today, Arjun maintains a ₹15,000 monthly SIP across three funds, checking his portfolio quarterly—not daily. The transformation was behavioural, not informational.

Or Neha, a 42-year-old entrepreneur, who had invested sporadically for years without tracking progress. After attending a financial literacy workshop, she instituted a 30-minute monthly "investment reflection session." She reviews performance, reassesses goals, and evaluates SIPs. The ritual has improved portfolio health and reduced anxiety. As she says, "I stopped letting markets define my mood."

These examples highlight a core theme: action does not require mastery—it requires momentum. You do not need complete knowledge. You need to start, observe, and iterate. Sophistication can follow; clarity emerges through doing.

Implementation is not the final step of investing; it is the first step of ownership. Information becomes action, theory becomes habit, fear becomes clarity. The abstract future becomes tangible, actively shaped, one SIP at a time.

Opening Your First Account (Step-by-Step)

Most people don't fail to invest because of apathy—they fail because of ambiguity. The modern investor is not short on information; they are buried under it. Platform ads scream for attention, financial influencers flood social media with half-truths, and even well-meaning friends often contradict one another. But behind the confusion is a surprisingly straightforward process. The key is clarity: knowing which steps matter, which decisions are reversible, and which are just noise. Opening your first investment account and setting up a Systematic Investment Plan (SIP) is not a mystical rite—it's a practical sequence of actions, no more intimidating than opening a bank account or installing a mobile app. Done well, it can take less than 30 minutes and fundamentally rewire your financial life.

The first real decision is *where* to invest. While mutual funds themselves are standardised across platforms, the *user experience* is not. There are three broad categories of platforms: (1) direct mutual fund websites (like HDFC Mutual Fund or Axis MF); (2) aggregators and investment apps (like Groww, Zerodha Coin, Paytm Money, Kuvera); and (3) full-service brokers (like ICICI Direct or HDFC Securities). Each has trade-offs. Direct AMC websites offer simplicity but may lack holistic visibility across funds. Aggregator apps provide portfolio-level dashboards, SIP automation, and minimalist interfaces, often ideal for new investors. Full-service brokers tend to suit more advanced investors who want equities and mutual funds in one place. There is no singular 'best'. But *ease of use*, *zero-commission access*, and *clarity of interface* should drive your first choice.

Once you've selected a platform, the next requirement is KYC—Know Your Customer. This is not a bureaucratic hoop but a legal prerequisite. Thankfully, most platforms now offer *e-KYC* or *video KYC*, allowing you to complete this step digitally in under 15 minutes. You'll typically need your PAN card, Aadhaar number, and a quick selfie or live video confirmation. Many platforms validate your credentials in real-time, meaning you can move to investing the same day. It's worth noting that KYC is *portable*—once done with one fund house or platform, it is valid across the industry. This means you don't need to repeat it every time you explore new funds.

After KYC, you'll be asked to create your investment account. The terminology may vary—some call it a folio, others a demat account—but for mutual fund SIPs, you don't need a demat account unless you also plan to buy stocks or ETFs. In most cases, platforms will simply assign a folio number when you initiate your first investment. It's not something you need to manage manually. What does require care, however, is linking your bank account. Your SIPs will be debited automatically from this account, so it's essential to ensure you have sufficient funds, proper net banking access, and, where required, UPI or auto-debit mandates approved.

Now comes the part that intimidates most new investors: choosing the fund and setting the SIP. This is where many pause, over-research, and get paralysed. But remember, *the goal is not perfection—it is initiation.* Start simple. If you're unsure where to begin, opt for a well-rated index fund or a large-cap mutual fund. These are typically diversified, low-cost, and suitable for first-timers. You can always refine your strategy later. What matters is building a habit, not scoring an immediate win.

To set up a SIP, the platform will guide you through three main decisions: **frequency**, **amount**, and **start date**. Frequency is usually monthly, which aligns with salary cycles and creates predictability. The amount should be meaningful enough to signal commitment, but not so large that it causes financial stress. A useful benchmark is 5–10% of your monthly income, though even ₹1,000 is a powerful place to begin. The start date is often best set just after your salary credit, ensuring liquidity. Once these details are selected, you authorise the mandate—either through net banking, UPI, or a physical form depending on the bank and platform—and your SIP is live.

At this point, it's worth discussing *mental models*, not just mechanics. The biggest barrier to starting is usually not the platform or the paperwork. It is the fear of doing something wrong, of not knowing enough, or of locking yourself into a commitment you're unsure about. But the reality is that SIPs are highly flexible. You can increase, pause, reduce, or cancel them at any time—often with just a few clicks. Unlike insurance policies or fixed deposits, they do not have penalties or lock-ins (except in tax-saving ELSS funds, which have a three-year lock-in). This makes them uniquely forgiving—and ideal for building confidence through practice.

Consider the case of Vikram, a 32-year-old architect in Pune who spent months reading about mutual funds but could never commit to a fund. The turning point came when he challenged himself to "just set up a ₹500 SIP" in a Nifty 50 index fund. That decision took 20 minutes. Within three months, he had increased his SIP to ₹5,000, diversified across two other funds, and was tracking his goals with a minimalist spreadsheet. The transformation was not informational—it was behavioural. *Action created clarity.*

Or Aarti, a 40-year-old schoolteacher who thought investing was only for people with finance backgrounds. With help from a friend, she set up her KYC, installed a mutual fund app, and started a SIP in a balanced advantage fund with ₹2,000 per month. What surprised her most wasn't the returns—it was the feeling of control. "Every time the SIP goes out," she said, "I feel like I've done something for my future that day." That's not an abstract idea—it's a neurochemical shift. Automating your investments creates a steady rhythm that reduces anxiety, fosters consistency, and builds confidence over time.

As a bonus, most platforms now provide **dashboard views** of your investments: cumulative SIPs, returns, fund health, and allocation charts. Use these monthly—not daily. The purpose is not to obsess over day-to-day NAVs, but to verify that your SIPs are active, mandates are working, and nothing has lapsed. If a payment fails, you'll typically receive an alert. But more important than any alert is your own *quarterly review*. That's where you check alignment with your goals, risk profile, and upcoming financial needs.

This is also where platforms differentiate themselves. Some allow "goal tagging," where each SIP can be linked to a specific objective—retirement, travel, education, etc. Others offer insights into fund overlap, tax optimisation, or rebalancing prompts. These features are not essential on Day One—but they become helpful as you grow more confident. For now, focus on one clean action: open the account, set up the SIP, and begin.

To summarise without summarising: *starting is not a technical act—it is a psychological inflection point.* You are shifting from passive observer to active participant in your financial life. You are taking control—not just of your money, but of your mindset. And that control does not come from having all the answers. It comes from taking the first step with eyes open, platform chosen, fund selected, and commitment in place.

No amount of reading, analysis, or theoretical conviction can substitute for the feeling of seeing your first SIP go through. That moment is the quiet start of something compounding—not just financially, but cognitively. You will not forget it. And you will never look at your money—or your future—the same way again.

Domestic vs International Fund Access

The notion that your financial destiny must be tethered to your country of residence is no longer tenable. In a world where capital, innovation, and disruption cross borders with the speed of thought, geographic diversification is no longer a luxury reserved for institutions or the ultra-wealthy—it is a rational imperative for every investor. The Indian economy, vibrant and promising though it is, represents roughly 3–4% of global GDP. To limit your investments solely within national borders is to deliberately exclude yourself from 96% of the world's economic activity. And yet, many Indian investors—often unwittingly—do just that. Why? Largely because the mechanics of accessing global markets have long been obscured by jargon, myths, and fragmented pathways. But that is changing. Today, there are clear, accessible routes to international investing, and they begin with two words: feeder funds.

Feeder funds are the most straightforward way for a domestic investor to get exposure to global equities using Indian rupees, Indian platforms, and Indian tax rules. In essence, a feeder fund is a mutual fund in India that collects money from Indian investors and channels it into a foreign fund—typically a global mutual fund, ETF, or index fund managed by an overseas asset manager. For example, the Motilal Oswal Nasdaq 100 Fund of Fund allows Indian investors to participate in the Nasdaq 100 Index via its underlying ETF in the US. Likewise, Franklin India Feeder – Franklin US Opportunities Fund gives access to high-growth US companies like Amazon, Google, and Tesla, without the investor ever having to open a foreign brokerage account.

The primary benefit of feeder funds is simplicity. They eliminate the need for forex remittance, international account opening, or tax complications around foreign holdings. You invest in INR, redeem in INR, and receive tax treatment similar to Indian debt funds (unless the fund invests more than 65% in Indian equities, which is rare for global funds). NAVs are declared daily, and investments can be made via SIPs or lumpsum, just like any other domestic fund.

Platforms like Coin by Zerodha, Paytm Money, or Groww all support international feeder fund transactions. The friction is minimal. The challenge is often psychological.

Too often, new investors ask, "Why should I invest in the US when I don't live there?" That question betrays a geographic bias. A better question is, "Where is innovation happening at scale, and how can I participate in its economic upside?" Whether it's artificial intelligence in Silicon Valley, semiconductors in Taiwan, luxury in Europe, or green energy in Scandinavia, global equity exposure allows your portfolio to ride the wave of industries and ideas regardless of where they originate. Feeder funds make this participation seamless, regulated, and increasingly popular among urban, salaried Indian investors.

That said, feeder funds are not without limitations. Because they are intermediated vehicles, there may be a time lag between when the underlying fund is valued and when the NAV is reported in India. This can result in minor tracking differences. Additionally, some funds may have minimum investment thresholds or restrict further inflows during periods of capital controls—particularly when the overall industry breaches SEBI's overseas investment limits (as occurred in 2022). Investors should stay informed about such regulatory caps, even if they don't often impact long-term SIPs.

Beyond feeder funds, the second path is direct international investing under the Liberalised Remittance Scheme (LRS) of the Reserve Bank of India. As of this writing, every Indian resident individual is allowed to remit up to USD 250,000 per financial year abroad for permissible investments. This route enables you to open a foreign brokerage account with platforms like Vested, INDmoney, or Stockal, and invest directly in US-listed stocks, ETFs, and mutual funds. Some platforms even allow fractional investing, meaning you can buy 0.25 shares of Amazon instead of spending thousands on a single stock.

The appeal of this route lies in *control and variety*. You can pick specific ETFs (say, the iShares MSCI Emerging Markets ETF), track currency impact in real-time, and potentially access asset classes unavailable domestically—such as US REITs or global thematic

ETFs (cybersecurity, space tech, electric vehicles, etc.). But this freedom comes with complexity. Currency conversion charges, TCS (Tax Collected at Source), double taxation agreements, and foreign tax filing obligations all need to be understood before diving in. For most new investors, this makes the direct route better suited as a *second-stage* move after getting comfortable with feeder funds.

Consider the example of Rajiv, a 34-year-old software engineer in Bengaluru, who began his global investment journey with a ₹5,000 SIP into the Mirae Asset NYSE FANG+ FoF. Over two years, he saw his exposure to high-growth US tech companies grow in a steady, rupee-denominated structure. As his salary increased and he grew more curious, he later opened a Vested account to directly purchase ESG ETFs and healthcare REITs from the US. Today, roughly 20% of his equity portfolio is international. What Rajiv understood early—and what many investors miss—is that *geographic diversification is not about predicting which market will outperform next year.* It's about reducing dependency risk.

Dependency risk is the silent killer of long-term portfolios. If your career, home, health care, and investments are all located in one country, your financial future is vulnerable to political, regulatory, currency, and economic shocks within that single geography. Even if India performs exceptionally well over the next few decades—as many believe it will—the principle of anti-fragility demands that your financial life shouldn't depend entirely on that assumption. Owning international assets is not a rejection of India; it is a commitment to durability.

From a returns perspective, the argument for global investing is not to find "better" markets but to create a smoother, more resilient overall return profile. For example, in 2022, while Indian equities held steady, US tech plummeted. In 2020, the opposite happened. Over 10–15 years, a diversified mix often yields a more emotionally tolerable investment journey, even if the average returns converge. More importantly, international investing can help you avoid the performance myopia that results from comparing only Indian benchmarks.

Taxation is a common source of confusion. Feeder funds in India are taxed like debt mutual funds if they don't hold 65% in Indian equity—which means indexation benefits for holding over three years (under current laws). Direct US investments, on the other hand, may incur capital gains taxes in the US and require disclosure in Indian income tax filings. However, India has a tax treaty with the US, which allows you to claim credit for taxes paid abroad, thereby avoiding double taxation. It is essential to work with a tax advisor if your direct holdings grow large.

Finally, let's address behavioural ease. Many investors intellectually understand the case for global investing but avoid it simply because the decision feels layered and abstract. One way to overcome this inertia is to start with a symbolic stake. For instance, a ₹1,000 SIP into an international fund—even if small—can create emotional familiarity. You begin to watch the global indices, understand currency trends, and track news with a broader lens. That small investment expands your mental aperture, making future decisions easier. *You don't need to go global all at once. You just need to start crossing the border mentally.*

Today, global investing is no longer a specialist's domain. It is a mindset that any informed investor can adopt. With the right mix of domestic strength and international exposure, your portfolio becomes more than a collection of funds—it becomes a resilient, future-ready ecosystem. As the world shifts from local to global in everything from tech to climate to economics, your investments should reflect that shift. Not for novelty, not for speculation, but for balance. And ultimately, for freedom.

How to Track Without Obsessing

There's a moment every new investor confronts: the temptation to check their portfolio after every headline, dip, or market rally. What begins as curiosity quickly morphs into compulsive tracking, with apps opened more frequently than one's email inbox. It feels responsible, even rational. But it isn't. *The paradox is this: the more often you check your investments, the less rationally you tend to behave.* Monitoring breeds emotion, and emotion sabotages discipline.

The challenge is not to track less, but to track better. The aim is to build a relationship with your portfolio that is rooted in clarity, not fear; structure, not instinct. This requires a shift from reactive checking to intentional reviewing. You don't need to be a passive spectator of your financial life—but you do need to curate the frequency, depth, and method of engagement. Because *obsession isn't a form of vigilance. It's a mask for insecurity.*

Let's begin with cadence. One of the most effective things a long-term investor can do is set a **fixed review rhythm**—and then honour it religiously. For most investors, a **monthly check-in** suffices. It allows for enough time to pass for meaningful movements to occur, without being so long that risks or anomalies go unnoticed. Daily checking is almost always noise. Weekly check-ins can work for professionals managing tactical positions, but for the typical SIP-driven investor, it's overkill. Monthly creates a balance—space to live your life, with structure to monitor your future.

What should a monthly review include? Not price movements, but *directional alignment.* Are your SIPs being deducted correctly? Are there any alerts from your fund house regarding rebalancing, scheme changes, or mergers? Has there been a change in your income, expenses, or risk appetite that would warrant revisiting your fund allocation? The aim of the review is not to react to markets, but to reflect on your *life's alignment* with your investment plan. Your money moves because your life moves—not the other way around.

To make this habit sustainable, use **automated systems** to remove both friction and temptation. Every major mutual fund platform in India now offers SIP tracking dashboards, email summaries, and app notifications. Configure your email inbox with a specific label or folder for "Investments"—so statements, NAV alerts, and KYC reminders are corralled away from your daily deluge. Use calendar software to block a recurring 30-minute appointment every month—first Sunday, 9 AM, with a cup of coffee and no distractions. This is your *Investment Hygiene Hour.* You won't always have major changes to make—but the ritual itself is what matters.

If you're someone prone to anxiety or over-attachment, set **smart limits on notifications**. Turn off daily NAV updates. Avoid following your mutual funds on social media, where fund managers post updates designed to generate engagement, not serenity. Install only one app for portfolio tracking—ideally your fund platform's own—and uninstall redundant ones. *Information is not always empowerment; too much of it is performance poison.* A curated data diet keeps your focus on the plan, not the pulse.

A critical aspect of healthy tracking is knowing **what not to watch**. Many investors make the mistake of comparing their fund performance to the Sensex or Nifty 50 every week. This is intellectually lazy and emotionally corrosive. Your fund may not track those indices; your goals are certainly not benchmarked to them. A better approach is to assess your progress in the context of your goal horizon: Are you roughly on track toward the corpus needed for your child's education in 12 years? Is your retirement corpus growing in line with inflation plus real return expectations over a 20-year arc? The scorecard is not market-based. It is *life-based.*

To aid this reframing, consider building or downloading a **goal tracker spreadsheet** that doesn't track fund prices, but milestones. For example: "Goal: ₹2 crore by 2040. Current: ₹15 lakh. SIP: ₹25,000/month. Expected CAGR: 11%. On track? Yes." Update this monthly. It transforms investing from a series of emotionally volatile data points into a *narrative of progress*. That, in turn, reduces the need to react to every 2% movement.

An underappreciated tool is the **automated alert system** offered by many wealth management apps. You can configure these tools to notify you when a fund underperforms its category average for three consecutive months, or when the asset allocation across your funds drifts by more than 10% from your target. These *trigger-based reviews* are far superior to impulse-based checking. They enable you to take action when something material happens, not when something merely *feels* off.

Of course, all this structure must contend with the most difficult variable of all: the human mind. The urge to peek, to tinker, to react—these are deeply biological. Investing taps into systems of fear, control, and identity. The antidote is not cold detachment, but conscious reframing. *Each time you resist the urge to log in and instead stick to your check-in schedule, you build a small muscle of financial equanimity.* It adds up.

Consider the case of Neha, a 38-year-old dentist in Pune who began investing five years ago. In her first year, she checked her SIP dashboard nearly every other day, making impulsive changes to her fund mix based on TV commentary. Her returns were erratic, and her anxiety constant. After a conversation with a trusted advisor, she created a new system: one app, monthly tracking, goal-linked review dashboards, and a simple "panic journal" where she wrote down every time she *felt* like reacting. Over time, the act of noting these impulses helped reduce their power. Today, she checks her investments once a month, rarely adjusts, and reports far greater peace of mind—even though her actual asset allocation hasn't changed much. What changed was her *relationship* to it.

The lesson is profound. *Most investors don't need a better portfolio. They need a better posture.* And posture is shaped by habit. Tracking without obsessing is not a single behaviour but a suite of choices: how often you engage, what you focus on, how you structure your environment, and how you interpret data.

Investing is a long-term act of trust—not just in markets, but in oneself. To build and sustain that trust, your system must be both robust and humane. Let the dashboard serve you; don't become its servant. Let alerts call your attention, not anxiety. Let your SIPs work in the background, while your life happens in the foreground.

Because in the end, *the best investors are not those who watch most closely, but those who watch most wisely.*

When and Why to Rebalance

Every investor begins with some version of a plan—a thoughtful allocation across equity, debt, and perhaps alternative assets. That plan reflects who they are at that moment: their goals, income, responsibilities, and tolerance for uncertainty. But life, by its very nature, is a moving target. *If your investments remain static while your life evolves, misalignment becomes inevitable.* Rebalancing isn't a technical tweak—it's a philosophical commitment to self-awareness in motion.

At its core, rebalancing is the practice of periodically realigning your portfolio to match your original or revised asset allocation. But framing it as merely a mechanical adjustment understates its significance. Done well, rebalancing is not about precision—it's about *integrity*. It ensures your money continues to serve your actual life, not a version of you that no longer exists.

Consider how easily drift occurs. Suppose you start your investment journey with a 70:30 equity-to-debt allocation, aligned with a moderate-aggressive growth goal. After a few bullish years, equities outperform, and your portfolio becomes 80:20. Without intervention, the portfolio now carries more risk than you initially intended. That extra 10% may seem like a reward—but it's also unplanned exposure. Rebalancing isn't about penalising performance. It's about *re-anchoring risk* to a level that you can live with, sleep with, and stay with.

Yet rebalancing isn't only about market movement. Life events often warrant recalibration more urgently than market events. A job promotion with a significantly higher salary may enable you to increase your SIPs and slightly raise your equity allocation, assuming your time horizon hasn't shortened. The birth of a child could shift your focus toward capital preservation or earmarked funds for education. Marriage might introduce shared goals and differing risk appetites, requiring the creation of a joint framework. Divorce or the loss of a spouse may prompt a complete overhaul of your asset strategy. *Rebalancing is financial responsiveness—it respects the full emotional and logistical complexity of being human.*

Too often, investors wait for chaos to force their hand. They react to crashes or booms, rather than proactively checking for drift. This is partly because rebalancing is counterintuitive: it often requires selling what's doing well and buying what's underperforming. That feels unnatural. But *disciplined rebalancing is one of the few free lunches in investing.* It's a systematic way of enforcing buy-low, sell-high—without relying on prediction or timing.

The question, then, is not whether to rebalance, but when. There are three defensible approaches. The first is **calendar-based**, where you rebalance annually or semi-annually on a fixed date. This method is simple, predictable, and ensures that you periodically take stock—literally and figuratively. The second is **threshold-based**, where you rebalance whenever an asset class deviates from its target allocation by a certain percentage (say, ±5%). This offers more flexibility and sensitivity to real shifts. The third is **life-event based**, where rebalancing is triggered by personal milestones: new job, home purchase, retirement, etc. The most robust approach integrates all three.

Take Anirudh, a 42-year-old IT professional from Bengaluru. In his early thirties, he adopted a 75:25 equity-debt split, with international funds accounting for 20% of the equity portion. For seven years, he followed a semi-annual calendar-based rebalancing schedule. But after switching to a government job with lower but stable pay, he reassessed. His goals remained the same—early retirement and travel—but his risk capacity declined. He rebalanced to 60:40 and removed the international component due to regulatory uncertainties and currency risk. The result wasn't just a more stable portfolio—it was a *more congruent life strategy.* Rebalancing gave him coherence between his money and his reality.

A common objection to rebalancing is transaction cost. Yes, there may be exit loads, capital gains taxes, or minor charges. But *the cost of unchecked drift is often far greater than the cost of correcting it.* Another objection is emotional discomfort—selling winners and buying laggards feels like self-sabotage. But that's precisely why rebalancing is effective: it imposes rationality on emotional terrain. It ensures your portfolio doesn't become a collection of momentum chases and forgotten dreams.

Importantly, rebalancing is not always about action. Sometimes, the right move is *inaction confirmed by inspection.* A quarterly or annual check-in may show that your portfolio is still within tolerable bands of allocation. That's not failure—it's stewardship. Rebalancing is not about constant motion, but about calibrated response.

Modern tools can assist. Most mutual fund platforms now offer asset allocation dashboards, visual drift indicators, and rebalancing suggestions. Use them as guides—not gospel. A platform might suggest rebalancing every quarter; that doesn't mean you should follow blindly. Your personal context matters more than software outputs. Automation can track, but *only wisdom can interpret.*

This brings us to the idea of **life-stage alignment**—an overlooked but powerful lens. Your twenties and thirties are typically accumulation phases; your risk capacity is high, and you have time to recover from volatility. Equity-heavy portfolios are often justified. By your forties and fifties, the focus subtly shifts to preservation and strategic growth. This doesn't mean abandoning equities, but it does mean a more balanced core. In retirement, the goal is sustainability, not return maximisation. Rebalancing in this phase ensures income flow and protects against sequence risk—drawing down funds during a market trough. Every phase demands a fresh look. *Rebalancing isn't a task—it's a philosophy of renewal.*

Finally, consider the ethical dimension of rebalancing. It signals responsibility—not just to your future self, but often to your dependents, your partner, your legacy. When you update your allocations, you are acknowledging change—something humans are famously reluctant to do. You are saying, "I see what is, not just what was." That awareness is the foundation of meaningful investing. Not speculation. Not FOMO. Not algorithm-chasing. But self-aware stewardship of financial energy.

To rebalance well is to be honest, patient, and humble. Honest about your changing life. Patient with the arc of returns. Humble about your inability to time markets, but confident in your capacity to adapt with dignity.

Because the goal isn't to have the perfect portfolio—it's to have a *portfolio that makes sense to the person you are becoming.* And becoming is not an annual event. It's an ongoing condition. Rebalancing is how your investments grow with you, not apart from you.

Chapter 10
The Art of Doing Less, Better

Simplicity in investing can feel revolutionary. Not because it is inherently difficult to grasp, but because it runs counter to everything we are trained to believe. In a world obsessed with optimisation—from fitness trackers to productivity apps—the prevailing notion is that more effort, more adjustment, more intervention always leads to better outcomes. Yet, in investing, particularly through mutual funds, the opposite is often true. Doing less, if done deliberately, can outperform frantic activity. This chapter argues for restraint: knowing when to act, and, crucially, when to step aside.

The irony is unmistakable. Investors today are inundated with information, analytics, and tools, yet the more we tinker, the worse performance often becomes. Studies by Dalbar and Morningstar repeatedly highlight the gap between the returns funds deliver and the returns investors actually capture. The fault lies not with the markets but with human behaviour—impatience masquerading as diligence. A fund might earn 10% annually over a decade, yet the average investor may see only 6% because they exited during a dip, chased a trend, or mistimed re-entry. Discipline, not intelligence, emerges as the decisive factor.

Durable wealth is rarely flamboyant. Consider those who quietly amass life-changing portfolios: teachers, nurses, mid-level managers. They are not geniuses; they are consistent. They establish SIPs, select broadly diversified funds, and, above all, leave them alone. Adjustments occur only when life necessitates it, not when headlines demand it. These are the "quiet millionaires." Their success is behavioural, not technical.

The urge to intervene is deeply human. Markets are noisy, every correction feels personal, and each rally tempts us toward faster outcomes. Yet these triggers are often illusions of control. Frequent action confuses noise for signal. True discipline channels energy into what is controllable—allocation, savings rate, personal goals—while consciously ignoring what is not, such as market cycles or global shocks. The less you believe you must act, the more likely you are to succeed.

Automation is not merely convenient; it is philosophical. Automating SIPs does more than simplify administration—it signals trust in a system you've built. Investments become habitual rather than heroic. Volatility ceases to provoke reaction; it becomes background noise. Habits, unlike heroics, scale. Like locking the door at night or brushing your teeth, automated investing embeds discipline quietly and reliably.

Modern investors are paradoxically over-equipped yet under-focused. Sophisticated tools, fund analyses, and simulations can induce paralysis. This highlights a crucial truth: the pursuit of the "perfect portfolio" is often a distraction. The notion that a precise combination of large-cap, mid-cap, hybrid, ELSS, and international funds will unlock superior returns is seductive—but largely illusory. Beyond a point, over-optimisation erodes psychological stability, while marginal performance gains are negligible. The behavioural cost frequently outweighs the technical benefit.

The best investors prioritise sustainability over perfection. They construct portfolios they can live with through uncertainty, that they understand, and that are consistently funded. Success is measured not by outperformance, but by progress and peace of mind. That clarity anchors them during periods of volatility.

Investing is a contract with yourself. The terms are patience, alignment, and commitment. Breaking it—through panic-selling, excessive tinkering, or obsessive timing—has costs beyond money; it erodes trust in your own judgement. That psychological toll is far harder to recover from than any temporary market loss.

Trusting time is not merely theoretical; it is a daily practice. Compounding is not just mathematics but a lesson in consistency. Sitting still while others flail is not passivity—it is stewardship. Duration, not cleverness, is rewarded. Remaining invested is the great equaliser, rescuing ordinary investors from the tyranny of perfect timing and revealing a deeper truth: success lies in doing the essential things well, for long enough.

This chapter emphasises purposeful subtraction rather than endless addition. It is about saying no to complexity, about seeking the signal in silence. You will explore systems that remove reliance on willpower, habits that align with long-term identity rather than short-term ambition, and strategies to resist the siren call of perpetual optimisation.

Ultimately, wealth is not built in one decisive moment; it is maintained through consistent, disciplined behaviour. The real mastery in investing is not over markets, but over oneself. That mastery deepens, clarifies, and strengthens when you embrace the discipline of doing less—and doing it well.

The Discipline of Staying the Course:

If investing success were a matter of intellect alone, the world's top wealth builders would be analysts, actuaries, or academics. They are not. Time and again, the most consistently successful investors are not those with the sharpest models, but those with the steadiest hands. This is not a romantic exaggeration—it is a statistical reality. Wealth, when viewed over decades rather than quarters, tends to reward the unflinching, not the reactive. The most transformative trait in long-term investing is not intelligence, foresight, or even strategy. It is *discipline.*

Discipline is not willpower in the dramatic sense. It is not bravely holding through every crash or making heroic bets during downturns. Rather, it is quieter, more architectural—a willingness to build a system once and return to it reliably, especially when emotion or headlines tempt you otherwise. It is the practice of making deliberate choices and protecting them from your own second-guessing. Investors who cultivate this kind of stability outperform, not because their funds are superior, but because *their behaviours are sustainable.*

Consider the story of Maya, a public school principal in Pune, who began investing in mutual funds in her early thirties. She chose two diversified equity funds and automated a modest monthly SIP. She ignored market news, avoided the urge to switch schemes during downturns, and reviewed her plan once a year—never more. Thirty years later, she retired not just with a comfortable corpus, but with minimal stress and zero regret. There were no tactical reallocations, no attempts to beat the market. Her secret was *emotional consistency*, not superior forecasting.

Compare that with a more "engaged" investor—Rohit, a mid-career consultant who watched the Sensex daily, moved between small-cap funds during bull markets, paused SIPs during recessions, and followed high-visibility YouTube influencers with zeal. Over the same three-decade horizon, despite higher income and greater financial literacy, his returns were meaningfully lower. The performance gap did not come from fund selection—it came from *behavioural leakage*. The real cost wasn't fees; it was *friction*.

This is not an isolated pattern. DALBAR's long-standing studies on investor behaviour have shown that over multi-decade horizons, investor returns consistently trail the actual performance of the funds they invest in—often by several percentage points. The discrepancy lies not in market volatility, but in human volatility. Buying high, selling low, chasing fads, pausing investments out of fear, or overreacting to a financial headline—all of these are variations on a single behavioural failure: a lack of internal control.

Staying the course, then, is not a passive act. It is an *active discipline*. It requires resisting not just external noise, but internal impulses. Investors often misjudge where the true threat to their portfolio lies. It is not market crashes, inflation surprises, or policy shifts. The primary threat is *themselves*. Not because they lack knowledge, but because they lack containment. The instinct to intervene—to tinker, tweak, shift, or abandon—arises from an unconscious discomfort with doing nothing. And yet, most of the market's rewards go to those who know how to do nothing with conviction.

There is also a cultural contradiction at play. In most aspects of life, proactive engagement is rewarded. The more emails we answer, the more we're seen as productive. The more hours we work, the more committed we appear. In investing, however, *activity is often inversely correlated with results*. The very behaviours that would earn praise in other domains—staying informed, monitoring frequently, reacting swiftly—can be corrosive in investing. This misalignment creates cognitive dissonance, one that must be resolved by redefining what success looks like.

To build that redefinition, investors must shift their focus from *external validation* to *internal alignment.* The measure of investing discipline is not how often you outperform the market or time the trend—it is how consistently you adhere to your own system. Are you acting based on principle, or out of mood? Are your changes part of a predefined plan, or reactive improvisation? Are you investing to grow your capital, or to soothe your anxiety? These questions form the bedrock of behavioural clarity.

That clarity enables a deeper kind of resilience—one that is rooted not in confidence about the market, but in confidence about *your approach to the market.* Investors who have internalised this tend to be unshaken by short-term turbulence. They see dips not as threats, but as inevitable noise. They trust time more than their ability to predict it. And because their discipline is internal, it remains stable even when external conditions change.

One of the most telling examples of this mindset comes from Ronald Read, a former gas station attendant and janitor in Vermont, USA. By the time of his death in 2014, he had amassed an $8 million fortune—entirely through consistent, low-cost, long-term investing in dividend-paying stocks. There were no aggressive trades, no MBA credentials, no hedge fund strategies. There was only discipline. Read was not chasing alpha. He was anchoring his identity in a quiet belief that small, repeated actions, left undisturbed, can build something extraordinary.

This belief is not a relic of a simpler time. It is *more relevant now than ever.* In an age of algorithmic platforms, financial influencers, and gamified apps, the temptation to intervene has multiplied. The average investor today faces more decisions, more stimuli, and more distractions than at any time in history. But with greater choice comes greater fatigue. The discipline of staying the course has become not just a virtue, but a shield—protecting investors from an environment designed to provoke reaction.

To cultivate this shield, investors must invest as much in their environment as they do in their portfolio. Automate contributions. Hide apps that encourage daily tracking. Create friction for reactive decisions (such as requiring a 24-hour delay before acting on a sell impulse). Schedule quarterly rather than weekly reviews. Surround yourself with evidence-based sources, not fear-based media. These micro-adjustments are not tactical—they are *behavioural architecture*. They help replace willpower with design.

Ultimately, discipline in investing is not a constraint. It is a liberation. It frees you from the false urgency of doing more, and allows you to focus on what actually works. It transforms investing from a performance game into a practice of stewardship. A good fund, held through good habits, consistently applied, can do far more for your financial future than any exotic strategy. But that outcome depends on whether you can resist the seduction of novelty, the mirage of optimisation, and the illusion that *more action equals better results*.

The most successful investors are not those who move the fastest. They are those who move the *least*—with intent. They understand that financial progress is not a function of intensity, but of *durability*. They build systems they can trust, and then—crucially—they trust them. The market does not reward brilliance once. It rewards *discipline repeatedly*. And in that repetition lies the quiet compounding of wealth—not just in money, but in peace of mind.

Automation as Identity, Not Just Strategy:

Ask someone who they are, and they might respond with their profession, their family role, or a value they hold dear. Rarely will they mention a habit. And yet, in the quiet spaces between self-conception and daily behaviour, it is our habits that often speak the loudest about who we really are. Nowhere is this more evident—or more consequential—than in how we manage our money. In particular, how we *automate* our investing decisions is not merely a mechanical convenience. It is a *mirror of identity*. Automation, properly understood, is not just a tactical shortcut. It is an ongoing expression of who we believe ourselves to be.

This idea challenges the conventional framing of automation in personal finance. Most resources portray it as a rational tactic—"set it and forget it", a hedge against forgetfulness or procrastination. But this view understates its deeper power. Automation is not merely an efficiency enhancer. It is a tool of self-authorship. Every time you automate an investing behaviour—whether it's a monthly SIP, an annual portfolio review, or a rules-based rebalancing trigger—you are, in effect, deciding what kind of investor you want to be *even when your mood changes.*

This shift from "do I feel like investing this month?" to "I'm the kind of person who always invests this month" is profound. It transitions your financial behaviour from being mood-dependent to being *identity-consistent.* And identity-consistency is where true behavioural stability emerges. Research in behavioural science, particularly by psychologists like Wendy Wood and B.J. Fogg, shows that when habits are aligned with self-identity, they become sticky. They are not forced through willpower, but followed through instinct—because breaking them feels like a violation of self.

Take for example the case of Arvind, a 34-year-old graphic designer based in Bengaluru. After years of inconsistent investing, driven by bursts of motivation followed by long periods of inertia, he reframed the problem. Instead of trying to stay disciplined through willpower, he decided to internalise a new identity: "I am a builder of quiet wealth." He set up an SIP into a balanced fund aligned with his long-term goals, created a recurring monthly email reminder that he would archive without opening (a ritual of quiet affirmation), and disabled all notifications from his investing app. The effect wasn't just behavioural—it was *philosophical.* Arvind began to see every automated contribution not as a financial act, but as an expression of the kind of life he was designing.

This is not an isolated insight. Identity-linked automation can reduce friction across a wide range of financial behaviours: emergency fund contributions, debt repayments, charitable giving, tax planning. But its psychological utility in investing is uniquely potent because investing, unlike consumption or budgeting, has no immediate feedback loop. You don't "feel" the benefits of your investments daily. Which means the motivation to continue must come from a deeper place than mere results. It must be anchored in *who you are becoming*, not just what you're earning.

And this is where many otherwise intelligent investors stumble. They confuse activity with agency. They think frequent decisions are a sign of control. But in reality, constant financial micromanagement often signals a fragile identity—one that needs reinforcement through action. The more stable investor, by contrast, is one who can *delegate to themselves*. By setting up rules and systems in advance, they acknowledge a fundamental truth: their future moods may not serve their long-term goals. Automation, in this view, becomes an act of humility—a quiet admission that their better self is not always the present self.

Some critics argue that over-automation leads to detachment—that it removes the investor from an engaged relationship with their finances. But this critique misses the point. Automation is not detachment when it's done *with intention*. It is detachment from noise, not from purpose. In fact, many of the most successful long-term investors report feeling *more connected* to their financial goals precisely because they are not constantly fiddling with their portfolio. Their attention is freed for higher-level thinking—for asking questions like "What am I building this for?" rather than "Should I switch to a mid-cap fund this month?"

Moreover, automation as identity serves a vital role in resisting the dopamine economy. In a digital age where financial apps, news feeds, and performance trackers constantly seek your attention, the investor who defines themselves through calm, rule-based consistency is practising *rebellion through restraint*. Every avoided check-in, every uninterrupted SIP, every boring quarterly review becomes a vote for a version of the self that is *immune to noise*. This is not apathy—it is *sovereignty*.

There's a broader philosophical point here too. In many spiritual and psychological traditions, the path to long-term growth is not dramatic transformation, but quiet integration. Who you are is not what you think about in moments of inspiration, but what you return to in moments of routine. Automation, then, is not a mechanised process—it is a declaration of *who you intend to be when no one is watching*.

It removes decision-making not because you are lazy, but because you are already decided.

This also has implications for how we teach financial literacy. Too often, guidance is framed around tools and tactics—how to choose funds, where to allocate, what metrics to track. These are necessary, but insufficient. What's missing is the anchoring layer of *identity formation.* Teaching someone to invest without helping them define who they are as an investor is like giving someone a compass without a sense of direction. The most enduring investing behaviours emerge when they are wrapped in self-concept. When someone sees themselves as a prudent steward, a consistent contributor, a long-term thinker—then every action they take is part of a larger narrative arc.

That narrative, once defined, can be protected by automation. It acts as a scaffolding for when motivation fades, when markets tremble, or when doubt creeps in. And it's during those moments—when everything in the world is tempting you to act—that your systems will hold the line. But more than that, they'll *remind you who you are.* The SIP continues not because you remembered, but because *you set it in motion as someone who cares about the future.* The low-risk allocation remains in place not because you didn't panic, but because you built in a rule that says "I trust my past self more than my current fear."

It's worth asking, then, not just what systems you've automated, but what identities they reflect. Are you automating out of convenience, or conviction? Are you using automation to escape responsibility, or to encode responsibility into habit? The answers matter—because they determine whether your investing life is a collection of tasks or a cohesive story.

Ultimately, automation is not the absence of action. It is action, taken in advance, by a version of you who had clarity. By choosing to automate your investing with intention and identity, you are not outsourcing your financial life—you are *securing its integrity.* You are shifting the centre of gravity from reaction to reflection. From strategy to self. From trying to feel motivated every month to *becoming the kind of person who doesn't need to be.*

And when investing becomes identity, not just activity, its rewards transcend returns. They show up in confidence. In calm. In the quiet satisfaction of knowing that your money is working, not because you're micromanaging it, but because you had the foresight to build a system that doesn't need you to. That's not just a good strategy. It's a mark of someone who knows who they are—and invests accordingly.

The Myth of the "Perfect Portfolio":

The idea of a perfect portfolio is seductive—elegant in theory, dangerous in practice. It plays to our need for control, our reverence for optimisation, and our anxiety about uncertainty. It suggests that somewhere out there is a precise configuration of asset classes, fund types, and allocation weights that will maximise return, minimise risk, and guarantee peace of mind. And if only we research a little more, read a few more expert opinions, adjust just one more percentage point, we might finally arrive. This thinking is not only flawed—it is often paralysing. The search for perfection frequently derails the very thing it claims to serve: effective, long-term investing.

What fuels this myth is not ignorance, but intelligence misapplied. The more analytical a person is, the more susceptible they tend to be. Professionals, engineers, data-driven thinkers—those trained to solve problems—bring that same mindset to their portfolios. But unlike engineering systems or statistical models, markets are dynamic, probabilistic, and shaped by forces no spreadsheet can reliably capture. The investing world does not reward precision so much as resilience. And resilience is not built by finding the perfect mix; it is built by choosing a *good enough* portfolio and committing to it with discipline.

Let's define "good enough" not as lazy or average, but as *fit for purpose.* A good enough portfolio aligns with your goals, time horizon, and emotional tolerance. It may not maximise every theoretical opportunity, but it optimises for what matters most: *follow-through.* Consider the investor who obsessively fine-tunes their allocation every quarter based on macroeconomic forecasts. They may appear diligent, but over time, their performance is likely to be undermined by transaction costs, tax inefficiencies, and, most importantly, behavioural drift. Compare that to someone who selects a broadly diversified portfolio—say, 60% equity index funds and 40% debt funds—and sticks to it for 15 years. The latter may not win accolades for sophistication, but they are far more likely to reach their financial goals.

Chasing the perfect portfolio often becomes a proxy for avoiding discomfort. It's easier to tweak an Excel model than to sit with the uncertainty of markets. It's easier to change a small-cap fund than to accept that volatility is inevitable. In this sense, the perfect portfolio becomes an emotional crutch—a way to feel in control when we actually need to *surrender intelligently*. Long-term investing is not about removing discomfort, but about *learning which discomforts are worth bearing*. And the discomfort of occasional underperformance is vastly preferable to the long-term cost of inconsistency.

There's also a historical irony to the myth. If you examine the actual portfolios of people who built substantial wealth through mutual fund investing—teachers, civil servants, small business owners—their allocations were rarely optimal by textbook standards. They often stayed in conservative or moderately aggressive funds for decades. What made the difference wasn't perfect selection, but unwavering contribution. They automated, ignored noise, and let compounding do the heavy lifting. Their returns were not extraordinary, but their results were—because they played a *different game*. Not the game of optimisation, but the game of *adherence*.

Even institutional investors, with access to world-class research and analytical firepower, rarely predict which asset class will outperform in a given year. The SPIVA (S&P Indices Versus Active) scorecards repeatedly show that most actively managed funds fail to beat their benchmark over 5- and 10-year horizons. If professionals with billions at stake cannot consistently outguess the market, why assume that a retail investor, reading online blogs and forum threads, can identify the optimal portfolio mix?

The deeper problem with chasing perfection is that it externalises accountability. It creates the illusion that there is a "right answer" out there, and that our job is to find it. But investing is not a test with a key. It is a practice—a set of repeatable behaviours anchored in clarity and values. The right question is not "What's the best fund mix?" but "What's the portfolio I can live with, contribute to, and trust *even when it underperforms for a while*?" That's a portfolio with staying power.

This is not an argument against refinement. Asset allocation matters. Fund quality matters. Expense ratios matter. But their role is not to eliminate risk—it is to shape how risk aligns with your financial reality. A young investor with a 30-year horizon may tolerate 80% equity exposure; a retiree might choose a more income-oriented balance. These are not questions of perfection—they are questions of *fit*. And the search for fit is qualitative, not formulaic.

It's also critical to recognise that your "good enough" portfolio evolves as you do. Life changes—income rises, families grow, goals shift. Periodic review and adjustment are healthy. But such reviews should be strategic, not reactive. If you're changing funds every time a market commentator shifts tone, you're not managing your portfolio—you're surrendering to it. A better approach is to build a core allocation philosophy—perhaps equity-heavy for growth, debt for stability, and a sprinkle of alternatives if suitable—and then revisit it annually with clear intent, not ambient anxiety.

There's a behavioural edge to all of this. Investors who accept "good enough" tend to act more decisively, experience less regret, and stay invested longer. Those chasing the perfect mix often become paralysed by overchoice, a phenomenon well documented in behavioural economics. The more options we have, the harder it becomes to choose. And the more we delay, the more we lose out on the one resource no portfolio can optimise retroactively: *time*.

The obsession with the perfect portfolio also distracts from what matters far more: *inputs over outputs*. How much you save and how long you stay invested are vastly more predictive of financial success than how your funds are split across market caps or geographies. It's more important to increase your monthly SIP by ₹2,000 than to reallocate 5% from mid-cap to multi-cap. But perfection-seeking investors often focus on the latter, neglecting the former.

In fact, one of the most effective antidotes to portfolio perfectionism is *automation.* Automating your contributions and review cycles makes you less susceptible to the urge to meddle. It anchors your decisions to pre-set rules rather than current emotions. And by reducing the number of decisions you make, it increases the probability that the ones you *do* make are meaningful. Paradoxically, automation frees you to think long-term because it eliminates the need for constant evaluation.

There is dignity in simplicity. A well-diversified equity index fund, paired with a short-duration debt fund, held over decades, and fed monthly by a consistent SIP, is not exciting. It won't win applause from your peers or likes on a financial discussion forum. But it *works.* Not because it's perfect, but because it's *executed.* The perfect portfolio is a mirage—shifting just as you approach it, always promising more certainty, more safety, more return. The good enough portfolio is real—it's tangible, manageable, and sufficient. And in investing, *sufficient executed consistently always beats ideal never implemented.*

The invitation, then, is not to lower your standards, but to *refine your definition of success.* Move away from the illusion of control and toward the practice of stewardship. Think less like a trader chasing edge and more like a builder laying bricks. The goal is not a flawless blueprint, but a structure that stands firm through seasons. A portfolio that reflects not only market data, but your temperament, values, and life stage. One you can stick with—through volatility, through distractions, through life.

And that's the real secret: the best portfolio is not one that wins on paper, but one that *survives in reality.* It stays invested, it compounds quietly, it honours your purpose. Not perfect—but personal, persistent, and powerful.

What It Means to Trust Time:

There is something quietly radical about choosing to wait in a culture that rewards speed. We are conditioned to believe that acting fast, making moves, and chasing the next opportunity is the hallmark of intelligence. Yet in investing—as in agriculture, as in parenting, as in architecture—some outcomes are immune to urgency. They belong to the domain of time, not talent. And to trust time is not merely a technical strategy—it is a philosophical stance. It is a decision to relinquish control in favour of compound effect, to let slowness shape value, and to accept that the most meaningful financial legacies are often invisible until they become undeniable.

Compound growth is one of the most misunderstood forces in personal finance. It is often illustrated using clean charts and exponential curves, yet few appreciate the psychological endurance it demands. In the early years, the numbers barely move. The portfolio grows in frustratingly small increments. But beneath the surface, something essential is happening: *momentum is being built.* Not just financial momentum, but behavioural momentum—discipline, detachment, patience. These are not soft traits; they are core to long-term success. And they are cultivated, not through market knowledge, but through temporal alignment. *The investor who trusts time begins to see returns not as events, but as outcomes of behaviour sustained across decades.*

Consider a monthly SIP of ₹10,000 into a diversified mutual fund yielding a conservative 10% annually. In the first year, the portfolio grows to roughly ₹1.26 lakh. In the second, it crosses ₹2.65 lakh. Modest progress, barely life-changing. But by the tenth year, the investment has crossed ₹20 lakh. By year twenty, it exceeds ₹75 lakh. By year thirty, it surpasses ₹2 crore. *Not because of complexity, but because of consistency.* The later years deliver what the early years could not—not due to better funds or market timing, but because time was allowed to stretch compounding to its full arc.

The difficulty is that this arc unfolds quietly. There is no quarterly excitement in watching a SIP debit your account. No adrenaline rush in staying the course while others shift strategies, reallocate funds, or react to headlines. But this is precisely why trusting time is so powerful—it operates beneath noise. It transforms a reactive investor into a strategic one. It allows personal finance to become *personal character*, expressed through restraint.

This principle is not abstract. It is mirrored in the lives of real investors whose names never appear in the business press. The school teacher who began investing at 25 and never stopped. The retired couple who never chased hot sectors but consistently added to balanced funds. The quiet millionaire who never bragged, never shifted allocations, and never missed a month. Their stories are not about timing the market—they are about *timing life*. And life, when treated with intention, is long enough to reward the patient disproportionately.

Yet patience is often framed as a passive virtue, something to endure rather than to pursue. In truth, patience is active. It is a decision taken again and again—to not interfere, to not tinker, to not mistake movement for progress. It requires intellectual humility: the awareness that we cannot predict short-term market behaviour, and that most attempts to do so degrade performance. But it also requires emotional maturity: the ability to hold discomfort, resist comparison, and find contentment in incremental gain.

There's a deeper, almost ethical, layer to this. To trust time is to invest not just in returns, but in legacy. It is to create value that extends beyond consumption and enters the realm of stewardship. A parent who invests quietly each month is not just growing wealth—they are modelling consistency. A young professional who sets up automatic investments and ignores short-term volatility is laying the foundation for a life governed by inner stability, not outer noise. These are not financial choices; they are identity choices. *And identity, once shaped around patience, rarely unravels in haste.*

This is why automation becomes not just a tactic, but a tool for integrity. Automating your investments is not about outsourcing responsibility—it is about designing for consistency. It allows time to work without constant permission. It removes decision fatigue and anchors you in a rhythm that resists market mood swings. Over time, automation reinforces identity: "I am someone who invests, regardless of what others do." That self-image is protective. It shields you from panic and posturing. It allows you to keep showing up for the slow work of wealth creation.

What, then, keeps investors from trusting time? Often, it is not information, but restlessness. The desire to optimise, to outperform, to predict, to do *something*. This compulsion to act is understandable—markets are dynamic, media is noisy, and financial goals can feel urgent. But the irony is that most action under pressure leads to poorer outcomes. Investors who check their portfolios daily are more likely to switch funds at the wrong time, chase short-term performance, and interrupt compounding just as it's beginning to accelerate. *Impatience is not just emotional—it is costly.*

To trust time, then, is to create conditions where discipline is easier than disruption. That means clear goals, simple portfolios, automatic contributions, and a defined review process—perhaps once a year, not every month. It means measuring success by progress toward personal goals, not benchmark comparisons. It means designing a financial life where *stillness is a strength*, not a failure of vigilance.

There is also a spiritual sensibility embedded in this mindset. Slowing down to invest intentionally is an act of self-trust. It says, "I don't need to prove my intelligence by doing more. I trust the process. I trust my plan. I trust the arithmetic of compounding." This is not naïve. It is principled. And it often outperforms precisely because it avoids the traps of cleverness.

When we examine those who have built generational wealth—founders, fund managers, patient families—what stands out is not their technical genius, but their *temporal patience*. They understood sequencing. They stayed the course when it felt unglamorous. They let boring assets do remarkable work. And in doing so, they proved a profound truth: *time is not a variable to be controlled, but a force to be partnered with.*

If there's a single takeaway, it's this: great investors don't just act differently—they think differently. They see time not as a constraint, but as an asset. They don't ask, "What's the best return this year?" but "What behaviours will give me the best outcome twenty years from now?" They think in decades, not days. And they build not just portfolios, but philosophies.

That's what it means to trust time. It's not about waiting passively. It's about acting in ways that only make sense in the long run. It's about investing with humility, patience, and purpose. And it's about understanding that the real yield of investing is not just financial independence—but psychological freedom. The ability to live with calm, to act without panic, and to know that your wealth is not the product of daily decisions, but of enduring conviction.

Conclusion

We inhabit a world where noise often masquerades as importance. Headlines scream urgency, dashboards promise instant clarity, and digital alerts compete for our attention. Yet true wealth creation has rarely depended on speed or volume. It thrives in stillness. And make no mistake—stillness is not passivity. It is intentionality unshaken by distraction. It allows the long-term investor to grow richer, not through constant motion, but through quiet commitment. The final lesson of this book is neither about picking the "right" fund nor executing the most precise rebalancing. It is about trusting silence over stimulation, patience over precision, and substance over spectacle. Perhaps the boldest act in modern investing is to do less—and to do it deliberately.

By the time you reach this chapter, you are no longer a beginner in the conventional sense. You understand NAVs, asset classes, and SIP mechanics. More importantly, you are reconsidering what it means to grow wealth meaningfully. This chapter is not a recap; it is a reframing. Every choice you make from this point—every rupee invested, every notification resisted, every moment of composure—becomes a statement about who you are and who you are becoming.

The metaphor of the tree—planted, nurtured, and left to flourish—is apt not for its poetry, but for its practicality. Most investors stumble not from ignorance, but from impatience. They uproot their saplings in search of faster growth or richer soil. Yet every portfolio has seasons. There will be stretches of apparent stagnation, periods of slow accumulation, and phases when progress seems invisible. Discipline lies in resisting interference. Across decades, the patient investor builds not only capital but also confidence—confidence in the process, the plan, and, most critically, in themselves.

Consider the weight lifted when you release the pursuit of perfect allocation, when you stop checking your portfolio daily, and when you begin to think in years rather than weeks. Performance anxiety—the heavy cloak fed by financial media and self-doubt—begins to lift. Without the constant need to "beat the market" or "optimise," you make space for a more enduring ambition:

consistency. It may lack drama, but consistency is the true currency of financial transformation. Quiet, steadfast investors often amass wealth not through brilliance, but through persistent adherence to their plan.

Automation transcends convenience; it is an act of respect towards your future self. By automating investments, you remove present-day temptation from the equation, building guardrails that maintain steadiness when the world zigzags. Automation declares: "The important decisions are already made; now I step aside and allow them to work." It is a philosophical shift from vigilance to deliberate delegation, enabling investing to become habit rather than hustle.

This final phase is less about acquiring knowledge and more about unlearning unnecessary behaviours. You need not respond to every headline, chase exotic funds, or overanalyse quarterly reports. The fundamentals—diversification, discipline, deferred gratification—remain constant. What evolves is your relationship with them. Simplicity becomes a strategy rather than a compromise, and "enough" becomes a more powerful benchmark than "more."

This approach is deeply human. Money is never just money; it carries identity, security, autonomy, and legacy. Anchoring your philosophy in stillness communicates the life you wish to lead: reflective, not reactive; measured not by metrics alone, but by peace of mind. A well-constructed portfolio is more than a compounding machine; it is a vehicle for restful nights, clear planning, and a life lived on your terms.

The purpose of this book has been to equip you with tools, perspectives, and mental models. Yet tools are only as potent as the hands that wield them. Real work begins after reading—when you implement your plan, automate your contributions, and step back. Not passively, but purposefully. Not because effort is unnecessary, but because time does the heavy lifting in investing. Complexity is not a virtue; resolve and consistency are.

Reflect on the early chapters, when investing felt labyrinthine. Today, it can be seen as a rhythm aligned with your values, goals, and temperament. Some invest to retire early, others to fund education, to build generational wealth, or simply to preserve independence. No two strategies are identical—and that is not a flaw, but a feature. The measure of success is a plan thoughtfully chosen, wisely executed, and maintained with calm even when the world around you does not.

Legacy need not be monumental. Its most profound forms are personal: a child who absorbs patience, a partner who feels secure in your steadiness, a life intentionally constructed that neither headlines nor dazzles, but endures. Cultivating such wealth does not require predicting markets or outsmarting professionals. It demands a far rarer discipline: steadfastness.

The ultimate insight is deceptively simple. You are ready—not because you know everything, but because you know enough and have the humility to let time work. You are investing not merely in funds, but in a way of life: deliberate, grounded, and quietly powerful.

Now, the action is clear. Invest. Automate. Step away. Let your wealth grow like a tree: resilient, rooted in decisions already made, nourished by patience and sunlight, unfolding season by season.

Invest in Stillness:

There is a profound discomfort that many intelligent investors face—not in choosing the wrong fund, or mistiming the market, but in doing *nothing at all.* In a culture that prizes speed, volume, and visibility, stillness is often mistaken for passivity, even incompetence. But the most durable wealth is seldom built in noise. It grows in silence—incrementally, patiently, and often without any external applause. The final and perhaps most underappreciated discipline in investing is not intellectual, but emotional: the ability to be still.

Stillness is not inertia. It is not neglect or indifference. Rather, it is a *calm confidence*—an internal anchoring that resists the constant pull of action for action's sake. It's what distinguishes the investor who panics at every market dip from the one who checks in once a quarter and then gets on with life. The myth of modern investing is that you must always be tweaking, optimising, updating, and responding. But what if your wealth doesn't need more energy—it needs less interference?

To invest in stillness is to accept that time is more powerful than skill. A mediocre fund held patiently often outperforms a brilliant one constantly shuffled in and out. This is not a romantic idea—it is a statistical reality. Behavioural finance has shown repeatedly that the gap between fund returns and investor returns is largely explained not by fees or product quality, but by timing decisions. In other words, most investors underperform their own investments simply because they *cannot sit still.*

Consider the quiet millionaires—the teachers, librarians, postal workers—who consistently turn modest salaries into significant portfolios. They do not exhibit extraordinary intelligence or insider knowledge. What they possess is temperament. They automate their contributions, ignore short-term noise, and trust the system they've set in place. Their wealth accumulates slowly but decisively. And their emotional discipline—rooted in stillness—is their greatest asset.

Contrast that with the high-income professional who reads every financial blog, reacts to every macroeconomic headline, and constantly reallocates in pursuit of marginal gains. Their returns are often unimpressive, not for lack of effort, but because effort was the problem. Investing is one of the few domains where doing *more* often leads to *less*. In most disciplines, input and output correlate. In investing, they don't. That inversion is conceptually hard to accept—but essential to master.

Stillness, then, is a posture of restraint in a world that incentivises reaction. It's not natural, but it is trainable. And it becomes easier when you frame investing not as a performance sport, but as a slow craft. When you realise that your portfolio is not a dashboard to be micromanaged, but a living system that needs *air*, *time*, and *patience.* Like a tree, it cannot be yanked upward to grow faster. It grows because you planted it—and then stepped back.

This philosophy also requires a redefinition of what progress looks like. Most people are conditioned to equate activity with improvement. In career, in fitness, in academics—more effort, more results. But in wealth-building, the real challenge is *staying with the plan*, not *upgrading the plan.* And that requires a shift in identity. You stop being someone who constantly evaluates and starts becoming someone who quietly endures.

To invest in stillness is, in many ways, to *trust yourself.* You've made the decisions. You've built the framework. Now your job is to let the process unfold. This demands not just conviction in your strategy, but humility about your limits. The market will do what it does. Your fund manager will have good years and bad. But your success depends on *your ability to stay the course*—not in theory, but in practice.

That means resisting the temptation to chase better funds every year. It means understanding that perfection is not just unattainable—it's counterproductive. The pursuit of the perfect portfolio is often a mask for deeper anxieties: fear of missing out, fear of underperformance, fear of uncertainty. Stillness asks you to sit with those anxieties and *not act on them.* To let discomfort pass through you without translating it into action.

Practically speaking, stillness can be designed. Automate your SIPs. Set a quarterly review calendar and stick to it. Unsubscribe from financial alerts that trigger unnecessary reactions. Remind yourself, regularly, that not reacting *is* a choice—and often the wisest one. You are not being negligent; you are being disciplined. And over time, this discipline compounds—not just financially, but psychologically.

There is also an ethical dimension to stillness. In choosing to grow wealth slowly, you are opting out of the frenzied, extractive mindset that characterises much of modern finance. You are building not for spectacle, but for stability. Not to impress others, but to free yourself. Your wealth becomes an instrument of agency—not dominance. It funds your values, not just your lifestyle. And it teaches those around you that peace and prosperity are not opposites—they are interdependent.

Philosophically, stillness aligns with deeper truths about how meaningful things grow. Relationships, reputations, skills—all of them take time. They require consistency, not brilliance. Trust, not tinkering. The same is true of wealth. When you understand this, your goals begin to shift. You move from short-term optimisation to long-term alignment. From chasing returns to curating a life. And your portfolio becomes a quiet mirror of your priorities.

Perhaps most importantly, stillness gives you back your time. It liberates you from the cognitive load of constant management. You stop living inside spreadsheets and start living outside them. Your wealth is not the centre of your life—it is the scaffolding. You live not to watch your portfolio, but because your portfolio is working, *you are free to live.* That, ultimately, is the promise of intelligent investing: *freedom from obsession.*

This book has given you tools. But tools are only as powerful as the philosophy that governs their use. Stillness is that philosophy. It invites you to trust what you've built. To trust time. To trust that enough is, in fact, enough. And to believe that you don't need to *do more* to *have more.* Sometimes, the most courageous act is to walk away from the tree—and let it grow.

Let that be the final, quiet takeaway: wealth does not need to be loud to be real. It can grow unnoticed, unmanaged, even uncelebrated—until, one day, you look back and realise it's there. Not because you chased it, but because you *allowed it.* Because you created space for it to grow. And because you learned the rare and transformative art of investing—in stillness.

About the Author

Julian Renner writes for those who crave calm in a world obsessed with hustle. With over a decade of guiding readers through the emotional and philosophical side of finance, his work invites people to rethink what it means to grow wealth—with purpose, patience, and peace. Julian's approach blends behavioral insight, long-view strategy, and a deep respect for simplicity. He believes that true financial success isn't just about numbers—it's about creating a life you no longer feel the need to escape from. When he's not writing, Julian can be found walking slow trails, sipping black coffee, and studying how ordinary people quietly build extraordinary futures.

www.ingramcontent.com/pod-product-compliance
Lightning Source LLC
Chambersburg PA
CBHW031346230926
51848CB00002B/407
* 9 7 8 9 3 7 1 7 7 4 7 2 7 *